American Toys

Other Titles in the Warner Collector's Guides Series

Available Now

The Warner Collector's Guide to American Clocks
The Warner Collector's Guide to American Longarms
The Warner Collector's Guide to American Quilts

Forthcoming

The Warner Collector's Guide to American Pottery and
Porcelain
The Warner Collector's Guide to American Sterling and
Silver-Plated Hollowware
The Warner Collector's Guide to Dolls
The Warner Collector's Guide to Pressed Glass

The Warner Collector's Guide to
American Toys

William S. Ayres

A Main Street Press Book

WARNER BOOKS

A Warner Communications Company

Copyright © 1981 by The Main Street Press
All rights reserved

Warner Books, Inc.
75 Rockefeller Plaza
New York, N.Y. 10019

🅦 A Warner Communications Company

Printed in the United States of America

First printing: March 1981

10 9 8 7 6 5 4 3 2 1

Library of Congress Cataloging in Publication Data

Ayres, William S.
   The Warner collector's guide to American toys.

   (The Warner collector's guides)
   Bibliography: p. 252
   Includes index.
   1. Toys—Collectors and collecting. I. Title.
NK9509.A97   688.7'2   80-25305
ISBN 0-446-97632-6 (USA)
ISBN 0-446-97974-0 (Canada)

Contents

How To Use This Book

The purpose of this book is to provide the collector with a visual identification guide to American toys and to supply descriptions of a wide variety of these toys to facilitate the collector's often difficult task of identifying and authenticating new acquisitions. To this end, an attempt has been made to classify toys (excluding banks and dolls, each worthy of a volume of its own) according to **clearly visible characteristics.**

Since toymakers throughout the years have consistently recreated the world in miniature, sometimes realistically, sometimes fancifully, the most immediate recognizable feature of a toy is its approximation of a particular element within the real world. Our eyes tell us what the toy is meant to simulate—be it a train, an animal, an automobile, or a carousel—long before we perceive anything else about the object.

This guide, then, consists basically of toys classified by **type:** wagons, fire equipment, streetcars, airplanes, dirigibles, boats, automobiles, see-saws, engines, etc. Because the toys included were all made in the hundred years between 1840 and 1940 and span a period that witnessed the transition from horsepower to automotive power, such major categories as wagons, streetcars, and fire equipment have been subdivided into both horse-drawn and automotive groups.

A second immediately apparent characteristic is the basic **material** of its construction: tin, cast iron, wood, paper, etc. Several large categories (trains, coaches and carriages, fire equipment, automobiles) have been further subdivided according to material—e.g., tin horse-drawn wagons and carts, cast-iron horse-drawn wagons and carts.

Of the fifty categories in this guide, a few have been classified by **function,** rather than by what the toys were meant to simulate in the real world. These include hoop toys (section 4), bell toys (section 18), automatons and other clockwork toys (sections 21 and 22), and optical toys (section 45), among others. These functions, like type and material, are clearly visible, even to the untrained eye.

Use of this collector's guide is designed with ease, speed, and portability in mind. Suppose you spot a toy fire engine that appeals to you at a flea market or in an antiques shop. At first glance it appears to be made of cast iron and is certainly a horse-drawn vehicle, otherwise unidentified. Perhaps the dealer has told you the obvious: "It is a 19th-century fire engine." But there are hundreds of 19th-century toy fire engines. Exactly what kind of fire engine is it? Who made it? When? And is it real or is it a reproduction?

By turning to the Color Key to American Toys (pp. 17-48), you will find among the fifty color illustrations a photograph of a fire engine that bears a close "family resemblance" to the one you're interested in; the fire engine, in this case, is obviously a pumper. Under the color illustration will be found the name of the classification ("Horse-Drawn Fire Equipment, Pumpers, Cast-Iron") and the page numbers in the guide that discuss and illustrate toys in this category (pp. 87-91). By turning to these pages, you will be able to find either the identical toy or toys similar to it, and you will discover, among other things, its maker, approximate date of manufacture, materials, assembly, mechanism (if any), and its means of operation.

Using this visual guide, then, is very simple. To repeat: once you find a toy that you want to identify, turn to the Color Key (pp. 17-48), find the color photograph that most closely identifies the classification of your toy, and turn to the pages indicated for further information.

Each of the 500 toys discussed in this guide is treated in a separate numbered entry, containing basic information. A typical entry is reproduced on p.9, together with a list of all the entities that are contained in each entry, from date and maker to mechanism and markings.

Included in the pages of this book are many toys that were manufactured abroad, particularly in Germany. These European-made toys are here broadly classified as "American" since most were specifically made for export and were frequently found in the homes of American children.

A Typical Entry

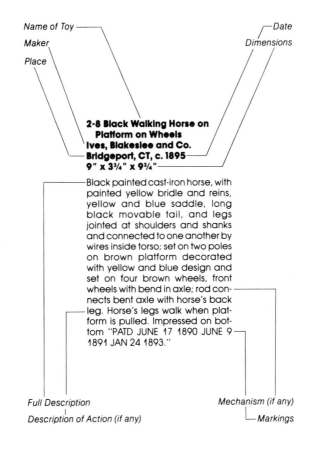

Name of Toy

Maker

Place

Date

Dimensions

2-8 Black Walking Horse on Platform on Wheels
Ives, Blakeslee and Co.
Bridgeport, CT, c. 1895
9" x 3¾" x 9¾"

Black painted cast-iron horse, with painted yellow bridle and reins, yellow and blue saddle, long black movable tail, and legs jointed at shoulders and shanks and connected to one another by wires inside torso; set on two poles on brown platform decorated with yellow and blue design and set on four brown wheels, front wheels with bend in axle; rod connects bent axle with horse's back leg. Horse's legs walk when platform is pulled. Impressed on bottom "PATD JUNE 17 1890 JUNE 9 1891 JAN 24 1893."

Full Description

Description of Action (if any)

Mechanism (if any)

Markings

Introduction

Manufactured toys sold in America during the period 1840 to 1940, including imported toys as well as American-made ones, are the focal point of this book. It is these toys which are the core of the American toy collector's world. Before this period there were few toys available in America which were made on a production basis; after this period there was such a change in the methods of production, sources, and quality of toys sold in America that the years following are the proper subject of another book.

By necessity a work such as this must be selective. Needless to say, not every toy—or even every type of toy—made during the 100-year period can be discussed. In order to talk about toys in any meaningful way they must be arranged into categories, and this involves selectivity and exclusion. First, as stated above, this volume is limited to manufactured toys or "production" toys—it does not include so-called "folk" toys or one-of-a-kind toys. And, secondly, because of limitations of space and the availability of other works on the subjects, this book does not cover dolls, dollhouses, miniature domestic items, toy soldiers, board games and puzzles, children's "working" vehicles, "box toys," or mechanical banks.

The first toys, presumably, came with the first children. There are, at any rate, examples of playthings made especially for children which date back thousands of years. Toys can tell us many things about the societies which produced them. They are indicators, first and most obviously, as to what children did, how they played and with what objects. Secondly toys serve to convey to us a notion of the values of adults in a society, especially their attitudes toward children—for adults, not children, on the whole, were and continue to be the makers and selectors of playthings. Thirdly, toys often mirror the development of their prototypes in the "real" world and help to show us the degree of importance attached by a society to the models after which toys are patterned. Finally, toys are in themselves indicia of the technical accomplishments of a society, as are all types of manufactured goods.

The above is true of American society in the nineteenth and twentieth centuries as well as of earlier and more primitive cultures. Through the toys which were produced for children we can see changes and developments not only in the numbers and varieties of playthings with which children were supplied, but also changes in the types of activities in which children were allowed to, encouraged to, and expected to indulge—as well as developments in manufacturing technology, in full scale and in miniature.

Why do people collect toys? Certain psychologists have suggested that the toy collector is often one who wishes to return to his or her childhood, to escape the pressures and responsibilities of being an adult. Though this view is somewhat extreme, there are undeniable elements of truth in it, for the collector of toys is indeed many times a person seeking knowledge of the past (and sometimes his or her own past) through the gathering of tangible objects from that past—but this can also be true of any other collector of old things. Nostalgia and history aside, the collector's interest may be primarily in the aesthetic or decorative aspects of toys, or in their mechanical functioning, or in the prototype which they represent, or in any number of other things about them. Whatever the motivation, however, there is one concern which the vast majority of collectors share: the need to know proper market value—for toy collecting can prove to be a substantial investment.

How does one determine the value of a toy? Again this depends on several variables, some of which will be weighed more heavily than others by each collector—and no two collectors will agree on the order in which they should be ranked. At any rate, here are a number of questions which the prospective purchaser of a collectible toy should ponder before trading money for it.

Is the toy a known production piece by a known maker?

The toy which can be identified by labels, marks, patent information, company catalogs, or other solid data is preferable, all other things being equal, to one which cannot. Second best is a toy which can be attributed to a maker by characteristic component parts, style or otherwise.

Is the date of manufacture of the toy ascertainable?

In general, a datable toy is preferable to an undatable one, and older toys are preferable to newer ones. Dates can be ascertained by use of catalogs, patent data, and so forth, if available, and can also be inferred by the general style and "feel" of the piece. A few notes of caution, however: many toys were produced year after year, and finding a particular toy in a catalog does not necessarily mean that its date of manufacture was the exact date of the catalog; patent data may refer to a patent which was several years—or decades—old when the toy was made; and as far as dating by "feel" goes, this should be left to the experts (there are certain toys which were made in the 1950s, for instance, which might appear to the novice to be nineteenth-century toys).

Is the appearance of the toy pleasing to the eye?

This quality can be broken down into several sub-categories: is the overall form of the toy harmonious and unified? Are its colors pleasant and do they go together well? Will it blend nicely with other toys on the collector's shelf?

Is there good mechanical design?

In general, a clever and complex design is preferable to one which is old-hat or over-simple. Many collectors are looking for examples of "industrial creativity" as reflected in toys. If the toy is in working order, very good—but if it is not, perhaps surprisingly, the price may not be significantly lowered: many collectors are satisfied merely to be able to see how toys used to work rather than to insist that they be in present working condition.

Are the materials and workmanship of good quality?

Materials should be suited to the uses to which they are put, and sturdy materials are preferable to flimsy ones. Toys with detailed and meticulous craftsmanship are preferable to those with lack of detail and to those where workmanship is sloppy or crude.

Does the toy convey a proper sense of its place in historic development?

This may be asked in two senses: (1) as to the history of toys and (2) as to history in the broader sense.

Is it rare?

Rare toys are preferable to commonplace ones in general. Note, however, that one-of-a-kind toys are avoided by most collectors since they are not "real" toys. To quote Louis Hertz, "The keynote of the collectability of a toy is that it was originally made and marketed as a commercial plaything." Special issue toys are avidly collected, however, as are variants (in form, color, etc.) and bona-fide errors. Also, some toys may be rare simply because few have survived from what might have been large numbers. This is particularly true of very old toys and of toys made of perishable materials.

Is the toy in good condition?

As assessment of condition of a toy depends on several factors: (1) whether it has its original finish and, if so, what shape the finish is in; (2) whether all of its original parts are there and, if not, whether the missing parts are important and whether substituted parts are correct; (3) whether it has been broken and, if it has, whether it has been, or can be, properly repaired; and (4) whether (if it is a mechanical toy) it is in working order, and, if not, whether it can be properly fixed (if the collector wishes it to work). Naturally, a toy which is found in its original carton with "like-new" original finish and all of its original parts intact and in working order is the ideal—but of course such a toy will rarely if ever be found. In weighing the several factors which add up to "condition," the following simple advice is given: avoid repainting or other alteration to the original finish (including its removal), avoid noticeable repairs, and avoid improper parts replacements ("composite toys").

Is the price of the toy in line with prices which similar toys are bringing in the current market?

The answer to this question is not to be obtained merely by consulting a "price guide" or by checking the results of a national auction, for it is difficult to tell whether the toy described is the same as the one in question, what condition it is in, and various other details about it. The most accurate way to assess correct price is to keep a close eye on toys as they are sold in the local marketplace (whether it be an antique shops, local auctions, flea markets, or whatever) and to consult with other knowledgeable collectors.

Is the opportunity to buy this toy (or a better one) at this price (or a better one) likely to recur?

If not, how disturbing will this be? One can agonize too much and try to weigh too many factors. And there are lost opportunities. So if the general feeling about the toy is good, if there are not too many problems with it, and if the price is not too far off, perhaps the collector should go ahead rather than be miserable worrying that he has missed the chance of a lifetime. This, of course, is the perfect rationalization for buying a toy which one really craves, but where the tangible factors above do not quite add up to a resounding "Yes." Perhaps, though, the prospective buyer should ask just one more question before taking the plunge. . . .

Finally: Is it certain that the toy is not a fake or a reproduction?

Well, is it? The answer to this question must be clear in the mind of the collector; no weighing is involved here (unless the toy is priced right even if it is not old). There are several distinct kinds of fakes and forgeries, including entire toys knowingly created with the purpose of deceiving the buyer into thinking that they are old and valuable, toys assembled from unrelated parts ("composite toys"), toys with false or obliterated markings, and so on. To be contrasted with these (but perhaps equally low in real value) are reproductions not meant to be sold as old toys (but which sometimes are) and certain modern toys with "old-fashioned" themes.

Enjoy the toy! (But think about it before you buy it.)

Part I Color Key to American Toys

1. Simple Toys, pp. 49-53

2. Horses, pp. 53-57

3. Other Animals, pp. 57-61

4. Hoop Toys, pp. 61-64

5. Horse-Drawn Wagons and Carts, Tin, pp. 65-71

6. Horse-Drawn Wagons and Carts, Cast Iron, pp. 71-75

7. Horse-Drawn Coaches and Carriages, Tin, pp. 75-80

8. Horse-Drawn Coaches and Carriages, Cast Iron,
pp. 80-84

9. Horse-Drawn Fire Equipment, Tin, pp. 84-86

10. Horse-Drawn Fire Equipment, Pumpers, Cast Iron,
pp. 87-90

11. Horse-Drawn Fire Equipment, Hose Carriages, Cast Iron,
pp. 91-94

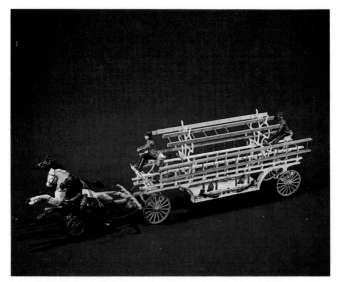

12. Horse-Drawn Fire Equipment, Hook and Ladders,
Cast Iron, pp. 94-97

13. Horse-Drawn Fire Equipment, Other, Cast Iron, pp. 98-100

14. Circus and Carnival Wagons, pp. 100-104

15. See-Saws, pp. 104-107

16. Carousels, pp. 107-11

17. Ferris Wheels, pp. 111-14

18. Bell Toys, pp. 114-20

19. Lithographed Wooden Toys, pp. 120-24

20. Automatons, pp. 124-28

21. More Clockwork Toys, pp. 128-32

22. Toy Engines, pp. 132-36

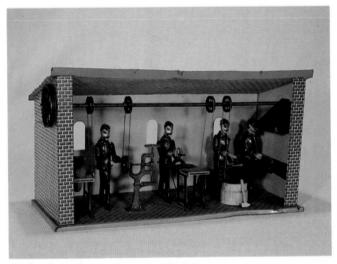

23. Engine Accessories, pp. 136-39

24. Streetcars, Horse-Drawn, pp. 140-42

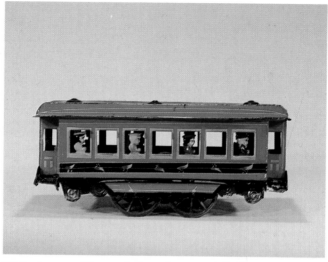

25. Trolleys and Buses, Automotive, pp. 143-47

26. Trains, Pull Toys, Tin, pp. 147-51

27. Trains, Pull Toys, Cast Iron, pp. 151-55

28. Trains, Mechanized, Trackless, pp. 155-60

29. Track Trains, Non-Electric, pp. 161-65

30. Electric Trains, pp. 165-70

31. Automobiles, Pull Toys and Friction Toys, Tin and
Stamped Steel, pp. 170-74

32. Automobiles, Pull Toys, Cast Iron, pp. 174-78

33. Automobiles, Clockwork and Wind-Up Toys, pp. 178-82

34. Trucks and Vans, Tin, pp. 182-86

35. Trucks and Vans, Cast Iron, pp. 186-90

36. Construction and Farm Equipment, pp. 190-95

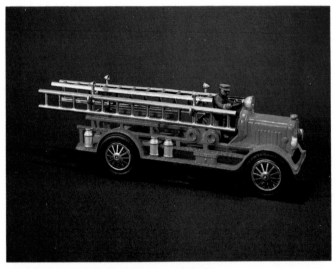

37. Fire Trucks, Automotive, pp. 195-99

38. Motorcycles, pp. 199-203

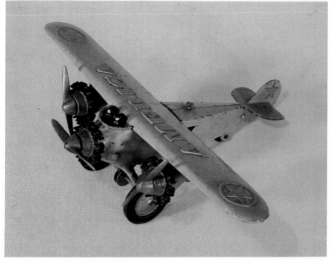

39. Airplanes, pp. 203-207

40. Dirigibles and Balloons, pp. 207-11

41. Boats and Ships, Pull Toys, pp. 211-14

42. Boats and Ships, Clockwork and Live-Steam Toys,
pp. 214-17

43. Cap Guns and Exploders, pp. 217-20

44. Artillery Toys, pp. 221-23

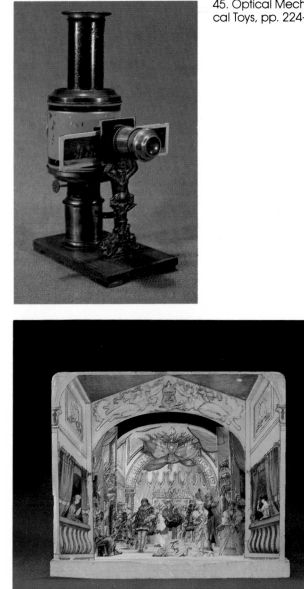

45. Optical Mechanical Toys, pp. 224-27

46. Dioramas, Panoramas, and Toy Theaters, pp. 227-31

**47. Historical Toys,
pp. 231-36**

**48. Comic Strip Toys,
pp. 236-41**

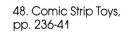

49. More Simple Toys, pp. 241-46

50. Extravaganzas,
pp. 246-49

Part II American Toys

1 | Simple Toys

As indicated in the Introduction, this book deals with production toys, not one-of-a-kind items or "folk" toys.

Of the simple toys illustrated in color, it is safe to conclude that several of them were mass produced—and it is even probable that all of them were. The maker of the top is **documented**, that is, its origin has been traced to a particular factory by the use of trade catalogs or characteristic markings on the toy.

The jacks are of a type which is found in significant quantities, and their origin and date can be inferred by reference to similar known toys and by a knowledge of the development of technology in the toy industry; there is some element of guess-work involved, however, and their origin and date are **attributed.**

Perhaps the most interesting toy of all, the jumping jack, has possible connections to a toy company in New Hampshire, but the information available is not sufficiently conclusive to attribute the manufacturer of the toy, let alone document it. Therefore, for the time being, its maker must remain **undetermined.**

On the other hand, some of the toys shown here probably **were** handmade, unique pieces—for instance, the balancing toy (1-1) and the church (1-3). It should be remembered that there are literally thousands of these non-production toys on the market and that they are legitimate collectors' items; they are sufficiently numerous to warrant a book of their own, and are shown here only to give a glimpse of this type of toy. (See also section 49.)

Finally, some of these toys are imported, and many other toys from Europe, primarily Germany, will be featured in other categories. They were an important part of the American toy market in the time span dealt with here—and are an important part of the collectors' market today.

These "simple" toys began to be manufactured during the early nineteenth century and continue to be manufactured today (though most of them now originate in the Orient). Some of them might be cited as prototypes for later toys—but the point to be made here is that children have found enjoyment in the simplest of objects over the years and continue to do so. Collectors, however, tend to find these objects less interesting than the more complex types discussed in the remaining categories.

1-0 Harlequin Jumping Jack (color plate, center)
Maker undetermined
Possibly New England, c. 1825
H. 12"

Clown figure, composed of flat-carved wooden pieces joined together with pegs, in conical hat, incised and painted in geometrical shapes. String passes through torso and is attached to limbs so as to move them when pulled.

Jacks (color plate, upper left)
Maker undetermined
Possibly Arcade Mfg. Co., Freeport, IL, c. 1890-1910
Two sizes: D. 2" and 1½"

Rough-cast iron jacks in star forms, six points each.

"Half-Dime Top" (color plate, lower right)
J. and E. Stevens Co.
Cromwell, CT, c. 1880-1900
D. 1¾", H. 1¼"

Cast-iron top, composed of disk with pointed post and string wrapped around post.

"For A Good Child" Whistle/Rattle (color plate, lower right)
Maker undetermined
U.S.A., c. 1850
L. 5½"

Tin drum rattle, embossed "FOR A GOOD CHILD" with American eagle on top and bottom and with alphabet embossed on sides, containing metal beads; whistle as handle.

Marbles (color plate, upper right)
Various makers
Germany and U.S.A., c. 1800-1910

Glass, china, stone, and clay variously colored, glazed, and painted.

1-1 High-Jumping Man
Maker undetermined
U.S.A., c. 1850-75
4" x 2" x 9"

Balancing wood figure of high-jumper, carved in the round, glued to axle between two turned black wooden pillars; balanced by turned wooden post with two lead weights glued opposite jumper on axle. Man turns around axle when weights are pushed.

1-2 Pecking Chickens
Maker undetermined
U.S.A., c. 1850-1900
H. 8"

Five wood figures of chickens, with tubular torsos and flat heads, tails and legs; set on wooden disk and attached by strings at necks to wooden weight swinging beneath disk. Chickens peck at disk when weight is pushed.

1-3 Church
Maker undetermined
Germany, c. 1850-1900
4¼" x 1½" x 8"

Red and white wood church with black painted windows and red door and minaret-type spire.

1-4 Monkey on a Stick Jumping Jack
Maker undetermined
Possibly U.S.A, c. 1850-1900
L. 15½"

Monkey, wood, head and torso carved in the round, with flat limbs jointed to torso by wires, and attached to two sticks, one a piston stick partially telescoped within the other. Monkey does handstand when telescoping stick is pushed up piston stick.

1-5 Walking Man on Stick
Maker undetermined
U.S.A., c. 1850-1900
H. 9½"

Unpainted wood man, with carved hat and face, and with arms, legs, and knees jointed with nails, attached at small of back to looped steel rod with wooden handle. Labeled on back " . . . McCAFFRE! MAKER SPRING . . . N.Y."

1-6 Dog-Headed Whistle
Maker undetermined
Possibly Germany or France, c. 1880-1910
L. 2"

Ivory whistle, in shape of dog's head with flat neck; ivory mouthpiece containing bead at end of neck.

1-7 "ABC Nine-Pin and Spelling Blocks"
McLoughlin Bros.
New York, NY, c. 1887
12" x 8¼" x 4½"

Eight blocks in form of nine-pins with alphabet letters made of polychrome lithographed paper on cardboard. Labeled "COPYRIGHT BY McLOUGHLIN BROTHERS NEW Y[ORK]."

1-8 Rooster and Chicks on Extension-Spring
Maker undetermined
Possibly Germany, c. 1900
3" x 6½" x 4"

Scissors puppet, composed of wooden extension spring made up of crossing grooved and flat slats held together with pin-nails; rooster and six yellow chicks, each made of flat-cut cardboard lithographed on both sides; set in individual grooves. Figures appear to move apart from one another to form a circle when spring is squeezed.

1-9 "Hello Express" Wagon
Maker undetermined
U.S.A., c. 1910
6" x 2½" x 1½"

Wagon, labeled "HELLO EXPRESS," of polychrome lithographed paper on wood, with hinged top and cardboard wheels, decorated with lithograph of children holding bundles.

2 | Horses

In 1840, the horse was surely the most important source of transport and power in America; by 1940, however, horses had been almost completely replaced by machines of one kind or another. The development of toys parallels this real-life development. The horses and equestrian figures featured here illustrate the three most important basic toy materials; tin (or more correctly, tin-plated sheet metal), cast iron, and wood.

The tin horses have several features in common with many of the other tin toys which will be discussed later: they are light in weight, relatively simple and two-dimensional in design, simply painted, and quite perishable—though not so perishable as the wooden toys (2-5). The essence of the cast-iron horses, on the other hand, is their durability and three-dimensionality, though some would argue that a certain charm possessed by the tin horses is lost in the cast-iron ones.

Note that some of these toys are animated; that is, they are made to move in a "lifelike" manner—some more convincingly than others (2-0, 2-1, 2-5, 2-6, 2-8). The techniques used to accomplish animation are sketched in the individual toy descriptions. These animated horses were also consolidated into more complex toys, many of which will be discussed in later categories.

2-0 Three Horses with Riders Trotting on Platform (color plate)
Maker undetermined
U.S.A., c. 1880-1900
11" x 5¼" x 9"

Three trotting painted tin riders (huntsman and two jockeys variously attired) on black, white, and yellow tin horses, respectively, each horse pivoting on axle between bow support and connected by rods at front legs to bends in axles; on green tin wheeled platform. Horses trot up and down alternately when toy is pulled.

2-1 Trotting Horse and Rider on Platform
Maker undetermined
U.S.A., c. 1850-1900
6¾" x 2½" x 6"

Painted tin horse and rider, made separately (horse of molded halves and rider of flat halves, both soldered together). Both are joined to rotating axle across inverted bow soldered to rectangular green platform on four wheels; horse's forelegs attached by hook joint and rod to bend in axle of front wheels of platform. Horse and rider sway up and down when toy is pulled.

2-2 Large and Small Horses Trotting on Platform
Maker undetermined
U.S.A., c. 1850-1900
8¾" x 2¾" x 7¼"

Large and small white painted tin trotting horses, both of molded halves soldered together, large horse with separately molded tail; set on wheeled green tin platform.

2-3 Large Pair of Harnessed Horses
Maker undetermined
U.S.A., c. 1850-1900
15" x 9" x 14"

Black tin trotting horses, made of two molded halves soldered together, with yellow bridles and orange saddles; soldered to semicircular support pivoting on axle between two large orange cast-iron wheels; connected to one another by triple-rod harness, and by long leather and canvas reins.

2-4 Large Horse with Jockey on Platform
Maker undetermined
U.S.A., c. 1850-1900
13½" x 5¼" x 11¾"

Brown painted tin trotting horse (molded halves soldered together), with separately cut orange saddle, soldered to green platform; set on four ornate cast-iron wheels; horse carrying jockey of flat-cut tin.

2-5 "Crandall's Lively Horseman"
Charles M. Crandall
Montrose, PA, c. 1875
10¼" x 4" x 16¼"

Flat wood acrobat, jointed with tin nails at shoulders and hips, attached by steel wires at hands to bit of wooden horse whose back legs are set on axle inside slot in wheeled box-stand. Horse rears up and down and acrobat bounces when box-stand is pulled. Printed on wooden label on sides "CRANDALL'S IMPROVED BUILDING BLOCKS" with patent dates.

2-6 White Galloping Horse on Stand
F.W. Carpenter
Port Chester, NY, c. 1885
6½" x 5" x 3¾" (horse only)

White painted cast-iron galloping horse, with rotating bit, molded bridle, collar, saddle and hip straps, and horizontally projecting prong on each side; red stand with gilt trim, two vertical braces to support horse, two black inner wheels with off-center adjustable horizontal blunt prong; set on four black wheels. Horse gallops up and down as back leg is lifted and released by blunt prong when toy is pulled. Labeled in relief on stand "PAT'D MAR. 20'83."

2-7 Horse and Rider on Wheels
Maker undetermined
U.S.A., c. 1890-1920
7" x 2" x 6"

Brown painted galloping cast-iron horse; set by two crude braces on four yellow wheels; rider, all brown, in cap.

2-8 Black Walking Horse on Platform on Wheels
Ives, Blakeslee and Co.
Bridgeport, CT, c. 1895
9" x 3¾" x 9¾"

Black painted cast-iron horse, with painted yellow bridle and reins, yellow and blue saddle, long black movable tail, and legs jointed at shoulders and shanks and connected to one another by wires inside torso; set on two poles on brown platform decorated with yellow and blue design and set on four brown wheels, front wheels with bend in axle; rod connects bent axle with horse's back leg. Horse's legs walk when platform is pulled. Impressed on bottom "PATD JUNE 17 1890 JUNE 9 1891 JAN 24 1893."

2-9 Workhorse on Platform with Wheels
Maker undetermined
U.S.A., c. 1890-1920
7" x 3½" x 5¾"

Black painted tin and cast-iron walking workhorse, with molded bridle, reins, collar, saddle and hip straps, and small-link chain extended from saddle through bit; attached at two feet to black tin platform on four small cast-iron wheels.

2-10 Walking Donkey
Ives, Blakeslee and Williams Co.
Bridgeport, CT, c. 1893
6½" x 2¼" x 6"

Painted dark-brown cast-iron donkey, with detailed molding, saddle and saddlecloth, and swinging tail; legs jointed at shoulders and shanks; holes at mouth for pull reins. Donkey's legs walk when donkey is pulled.

3 | Other Animals

Other animals besides horses were also found in toy form, of course. As a matter of fact, the variety is staggering.

The dog illustrated in color (3-0) represents the beginning point—unanimated simplicity in tin, very similar to some of the horses in the previous category. The cast-iron grasshoppers (3-8) are a later development with all of the pluses and minuses that cast-iron manufacture entails.

The wooden animals (3-5) deserve special mention. Those illustrated here are part of an elaborate set of toys known as "The Humpty Dumpty Circus," made by A. Schoenhut Co. of Philadelphia, which was extraordinarily popular. The animals were sturdily made and featured multi-jointed limbs so that the animals could be made to assume many positions. The set was originally patented in 1903 and continued to be made, in two sizes, into the 1930s. These toys can be found on the market today, often in good condition. The collector should be familiar, however, with the construction techniques, paints, and other materials used, since these toys are easily susceptible to alteration or "improvement."

In this category we have the first appearance of two relatively sophisticated animating machineries—wind-up and clockwork mechanisms. The former is typically composed of a spring or springs and a key with which the mechanism is wound; the uncoiling of the spring then propels the toy. Clockwork is exactly what the name implies—a mechanism similar to that found in mechanical clocks, often rather complicated but very powerful and versatile. (In either case, when the collector comes across the wind-up or clockwork toy, the mechanism is likely to be nonfunctional; it is up to the individual as to whether this is a concern. Many collectors simply do not care and, oddly enough, this factor does not enter into the pricing of old toys to a great extent.)

The German clockwork toys tend to be the most innovative and interesting. The Ernst Plank fish (3-4) actually swims in water and the un-illustrated goose (3-7) honks and struts realistically. Further developments in mechanical toys will be seen in many categories following.

3-O Large Black Setter on Platform (color plate)
Maker undetermined
U.S.A., c. 1850-1900
14½" x 6" x 14"

Black painted tin dog (detailed molded halves soldered together), with orange collar, separately molded ears and tail, and painted eyes, brows and mouth; soldered to green painted tin platform; set on four cast-iron wheels.

3-1 Dog Cart with Canine Bowling Pins
Maker undetermined
Germany, c. 1870-1900
21" x 6" x 12½"

Papier-mâché dog cart in shape of lying terrier, containing eight papier-mâché bowling pins in shapes of upright dog "schoolboys," set on wooden drums; approximately 6¼" high each. "Schoolboys" are of various dog breeds and are accompanied by a hound "teacher" in coat, tie, and spectacles.

3-2 Kicking Frogs
Maker undetermined
U.S.A., c. 1880
7½" x 4" x 7"

Two green and yellow lead frogs, standing upright and facing one another, each with one movable leg which is hooked by rod to bend in axle beneath pea-green platform on four iron wheels. Frogs kick one another when toy is pulled.

3-3 Cat with Rats in Cage
Maker undetermined
Possibly Germany, c. 1890-1910
8¾" x 2¼" x 6¼"

Yellow cat, upright on wheels, pushing cage containing two rats on wires connected to wheels of cage; barrel and spring mechanism beneath cage. Cat pushes cage and rats move up and down alternately when mechanism is wound.

3-4 Fish with Propeller and Box
Ernst Plank
Nuremberg, Germany, c. 1900
L. 9¼"

Tin fish with blue and white scales, pink and white gills, gilt eyes and fins, and tail connected by brace rods to body with rotating gilt propeller between; clockwork inside fish. Fish swims in water when clockwork is wound. Labeled on fish and box "E.P." with insignia of wings on wheel.

3-5 Schoenhut's Humpty Dumpty Circus Animals
A. Schoenhut Co.
Philadelphia, PA, c. 1905-30
Various sizes

A selection of animals from this extraordinarily popular set. Each consists of a wooden body, rubber cord jointed limbs and glass eyes, with various details such as leather ears and rope tails, all colorfully painted.

3-6 "Butterfly Push Toy"
Gibbs Mfg. Co.
Canton, OH, c. 1915
6″ x 9″ x 5¼″

Tin butterfly, with lithographed papered wings and molded red, green, and black torso, connected by rods to axle between two cast-iron wheels. Butterfly's wings, connected to torso by hinges, flutter when toy is pushed. Labeled "PATENT APPLIED FOR."

3-7 Goose
Maker undetermined
Possibly Germany, c. 1920
L. 6½″, H. 6″

Yellow tin goose, made in two pieces, neck and body, each made of molded halves soldered together, with steel rod legs soldered to torso; neck attached by hook joints to paper and wood bellows and clock-work inside torso. Goose shifts neck from side to side and bellows squeak when clockwork is wound.

3-8 Chirping Grasshopper on Wheels (left)
Hubley Mfg. Co.
Lancaster, PA, c. 1928
11¾″ x 3¾″ x 4¼″

Green cast-iron grasshopper, with incised detail, green wire feelers, black eyes, and two front legs jointed at chin and two back legs jointed at chest and knees; set at head on two rubber wheels and at belly on rubber tire; flexible steel strip extending from belly to semi-gear on front axle. Grasshopper's legs move and steel strip hits semi-gear to make chirping noise when toy is pulled.

Grasshopper on Wheels (right)
Maker undetermined
U.S.A., c. 1930
4¼" x 1½" x 1¾"

Nickel-plated and painted cast-iron green grasshopper, incised with detail, with nickel-plated legs moving up and down; lopsided wheel in stomach; set on two small front wheels.

3-9 Dog on Platform with Wheels
Maker undetermined
U.S.A., c. 1930
3¾" x 1¾" x 2½"

Black and white cast-iron dog, soldered to brown platform on four small wheels.

4 | Hoop Toys

These toys represent an attempt to achieve lifelike action in tin toys featuring animal and human figures, an attribute which they had formerly lacked for the most part. The basic design, illustrated in color, consists of a circular flat tin ring with metal strips stretched across its diameter and another metal strip between the first two at the center of the circle on which a figure, most commonly a horse, is suspended and is held in an upright position by gravity. When the hoop is rolled the suspended figure remains basically erect but pivots on its metal axle, bobbing back and forth, activated by the rolling motion.

The typical hoop toy figure is created in the same way as the tin horses and other animals mentioned in previous categories—that is, stamped or cut out of sheets of tin-plated steel, formed over three-dimensional wooden molds and corresponding halves clasped together; they are characteristically hand-painted. Some of the more elaborate forms typically include human figures (sometimes on horseback and sometimes dressed in cloth costumes), clock-work mechanisms to add additional life and interest to the toy, patriotic themes—and some rather bizarre attempts to use the hoop device in more innovative ways (4-5).

These toys reached their peak in popularity in the 1870s when most American tin toy manufacturers carried them in their lines. The New York firm of Althof, Bergmann developed the form to its highest degree of sophistication during this period, and Stevens and Brown of Cromwell, Connecticut, also produced notable examples including some with cast-iron double hoops (4-2). It is interesting that very few of this type of toy appear to have been made in Europe; they are almost exclusively an American phenomenon. David Pressland, the noted English collector and author, has said of them that "they epitomise the grace and charm of nineteenth-century American tin toys."

This category is one where the collector must be vigilant to detect alterations, repairs, and outright fakes. The toys are relatively simple in concept but, as noted, most alluring in their naive charm. Also, they are relatively rare. This combination of factors makes it worth the while of an unscrupulous person to use his ingenuity to produce a replica of an antique hoop toy or to "improve" one of the more ordinary varieties into something more exotic. Collector, beware!

4-O Horse in Hoop (color plate, right)
Possibly Merriam Mfg. Co.
Durham, CT, c. 1870
D. 7¾", W. 1½"

Painted and varnished tin trotting white horse (molded halves soldered together); rotating on axle between two parallel tin tubes extended across red painted and varnished tin hoop. Horse appears to run when hoop is rolled.

Horse in Hoop (color plate, left)
Possibly Merriam Mfg. Co.
Durham, CT, c. 1870
D. 7½", W. 1½"

Painted and varnished tin trotting white horse (molded halves soldered together); rotating on axle between two parallel tin tubes extended across blue painted and varnished tin hoop. Horse appears to run when hoop is rolled.

4-1 Hoop-Drawn Buggy
Althof, Bergmann and Co.
New York, NY, c. 1870
15½" x 4¾" x 10"

Red tin buggy, with figures of standing boy and seated woman holding baby, attached by steel shafts to red tin hoop containing tin trotting horse (molded halves clasped together). Clockwork mechanism located beneath footrest of buggy causes it to roll forward and keeps horse in horizontal position within hoop. Buggy rolls forward and axle-casing rotates to keep horse horizontal when clockwork is wound.

4-2 Boy Holding Flag and Riding Hoop
Stevens & Brown Mfg. Co.
Cromwell, CT, c. 1872
8" x 3¾" x 10" (without flag); figure: H. 9"

Hoop toy, composed of two different-sized red iron hoops with three spokes; set on axle with brass and steel clockwork in blue tin casing with open sides, supporting boy with cloth composition head and wooden torso with linen arms and gilt tin gloves and legs, dressed in cloth cap, shirt, and knickers, carrying linen U.S. flag on wooden pole in gilt tin holder. Stenciled on casing in gilt "PATd JUNE 25th 1872."

4-3 Circus Horse and Performer in Hoop
Althof, Bergmann and Co.
New York, NY, c. 1875
D. 9", W. 1¼"

Painted and gilded cast-iron and tin circus act composed of two gilt flat-cut tin half-horses on either side of clockwork mechanism, suspended from axle between rods across diameter on either side of red tin hoop; hanging circus performer, bare to waist, standing on top of saddle over horses. Stenciled "Wm Seller PATENT Sept 12th 1871."

4-4 Boy Carrying U.S. Flag on Hoop Wheels
Possibly George W. Brown and Co.
Forestville, CT, c. 1878
8" x 4" x 10¾"

Cast-iron and painted tin boy (molded halves soldered together), dressed in brown knickers, red jacket, and black hat and boots, carrying detachable flag; soldered to oval clockwork case, blue tin with gold stenciling, on axle between two large red cast-iron hoop-wheels of slightly different sizes. Toy runs in circle when clockwork is wound. Stenciled "PAT JUNE [?] 25 [?] 1878 [?]."

4-5 Leap-Frogs
Patented by William X. Stevens
Washington, DC, c. 1883
4" x 2½" x 5"

Pair of lead frogs suspended in large ornately cut gilt iron wheels supporting parallel pair of iron rods with wooden stops and copper frame. When toy is pulled by frame, frogs "leap" over one another. Embossed on underside of each frog "PAT. MCH. 20. 83. PAT. APR. 24. 83."

4-6 "Zick-Zack" Amusement Car
E.P. Lehmann
Brandenburg, Germany, c. 1907
D. 5", W. 3¼"

Steel and lithographed tin amusement-ride car set on axle between two large wheels, seating two passengers. Steel barrel and spring mechanism under cylindrical cover causes toy to roll; car continues in horizontally suspended position. Key impressed "LEHMANN" and "D.R.P."

5 | Horse-Drawn Wagons and Carts, Tin

Simple workaday wagons, carts, and vans were among the most popular of tin toys from the 1830s, when tin toys first began to be produced in quantity, well through the end of the nineteenth century. These toys convey, in a very immediate way, the value of work and thrift of those years and also demonstrate the appealing results which can be achieved through extremely simple forms and limited materials.

With rare exceptions (5-2), these toys were not made to be merely pretty or "just for fun"; rather they represented, in miniature, some aspect of everyday life depicted in an almost realistic way, unexaggerated but rarely humdrum. These wagons, carts, and vans were the "basic" horse-drawn tin toys. Their materials are simple thin tin-plated sheets of steel, paint, and an occasional cast-iron addition. The techniques involved are normally limited to cutting, stamping, bending, forming over molds, and soldering of the tin. The paint was applied by hand with a brush or by simple stenciling; the colors are typically bright and cheerful. The resulting toys, pulled by the type of simple two-halved tin horses which we have seen in earlier categories, have an immediate and direct appeal and to a great extent can document the ways of work in the period in which they were made. Most of them speak for themselves, often with labels painted on them, and there is usually very little doubt as to what they were intended to represent. Many American (and some foreign) companies, small shops, and even individuals turned out toys of this type in great quantity. Most of them on the market, with certain exceptions, are unlabeled and many of these toys must go without positive identification. Company catalogs, advertisements, and other aids do, however, allow attribution of manufacturer in some cases. The important exception to the usual lack of markings is James Fallows & Co. of Philadelphia whose toys are often marked "IXL" ("I excel!").

The collector should be wary of repainting, replacement of horses and wheels, modern "improvements," and outright fakery. These are fragile objects, and it is remarkable that so many genuine ones have survived in good condition. Many have not, however, and the collector must often ask himself whether he wishes to acquire a tin toy in less than pristine shape or whether he wishes to pass up what may be his only opportunity ever to own such a toy. Each collector must formulate his own approach to this basic problem.

5-O "Fine Groceries" Van (color plate, right)
Maker undetermined
U.S.A., c. 1850-1900
12" x 3¼" x 6¾"

Orange, green, and black tin delivery van. Stenciled in gilt "FINE GROCERIES," bent at center with open front and back; set on four iron wheels; connected by tin shafts to trotting white horse (molded halves soldered together).

Gilded Bow Cart (color plate, left)
Maker undetermined
U.S.A., c. 1850-1900
11" x 3" x 5½"

Brown and green painted tin cart, with three gilded bows, open front
and back; set on two cast-iron wheels; connected by double and rod
harness to trotting white horse (molded tin halves soldered together),
mounted on bent disk.

5-1 Dumping "Coal" Cart
Maker undetermined
U.S.A., c. 1850-1900
13" x 3½" x 5¼"

Coal cart with open back,
painted orange and gilded, labeled in stencil "COAL," soldered
to chassis rotating on axle with two
iron wheels; connected by double rod harness to trotting brown
horse (molded tin halves clasped
together); cart hinged horizontally
to harness by pin joint. Cart releases to dump backward when
pin is removed from hinge.

5-2 Cart with Filigree Sides
Maker undetermined
U.S.A., c. 1850-1900
17" x 4¼" x 7¼"

Painted tin cart, with four-sided
red base, three imitation filigree
openwork sides with blue rims and
open back; set on two iron black
wheels; connected by partly
pivoting curved shafts to trotting
brown horse.

5-3 "Pure Milk" Surrey
Maker undetermined
U.S.A., c. 1850-1900
14½" x 4" x 5½"

Tin surrey, painted chocolate-brown, stenciled in gold "PURE MILK,"
with gingerbread border along roof; two vats with covers; set on four
iron wheels, with driver; van connected by double rod harness to trot-

ting white horse (two molded tin halves soldered together) with two legs soldered to small platform with wheel. Horse labeled "No. 162."

5-4 "Pure Milk" Van
Maker undetermined
U.S.A., c. 1850-1900
12" x 3½" x 6"

Painted red and gilt van, stenciled in gold "PURE MILK," open front and back, green bent tin seat between windows; set on four iron wheels; connected by double rod harness to trotting brown horse (molded tin halves soldered together).

5-5 "Pure Milk" Wagon
Maker undetermined
U.S.A., c. 1850-1900
15½" x 4½" x 6¾"

Orange painted tin wagon, with turquoise-green interior, stenciled in gilt on both sides "PURE MILK"; set on four iron wheels; driver (flat tin halves soldered together) and two trotting horses (molded white tin halves soldered together), each horse with one back foot on iron hoop-support (with tab on back axle and brace beneath cart for ringing bell).

5-6 "Philadelphia Express" Wagon
Maker undetermined
U.S.A., c. 1900
12¼" x 5¾" x 7½"

Red tin wagon, stenciled in gilt on cream-white and blue-bordered panel on each side "PHILADELPHIA EXPRESS," with black striping, gingerbread-perforated sides and semicircular embossed shaft-plate at front; set on four large black iron wheels with steel axles (back wheels larger).

5-7 "Confectionery" Wagon
Maker undetermined
U.S.A., c. 1850-1900
14½" x 4½" x 6½"

Red painted tin wagon, stenciled on both sides "CONFECTIONERY," with black and yellow quarter-rotating hood; set on four iron wheels; connected by triple steel shafts to two trotting white horses (molded tin halves soldered together).

5-8 Orange "Express" Wagon
Maker undetermined
U.S.A., c. 1850-1900
10" x 3" x 3¾"

Orange and white painted tin wagon, stenciled "EXPRESS," with curved seat and high mudguard; set on four black iron wheels; connected by steel shafts to trotting white horse (molded tin halves soldered together).

5-9 "Express" Wagon
Maker undetermined
U.S.A., c. 1850-1900
25½" x 6½" x 7½"

Red and green painted tin wagon, stenciled in gilt "EXPRESS," with bench and four iron wheels; pulled by a pair of trotting brown tin horses; set on platform with two iron wheels; soldered to three shafts meeting at point in front of horses.

5-10 "Fancy Goods Toys" Peddling Van
Maker undetermined
U.S.A., c. 1850-1900
21¼" x 6¾" x 10½"

Green, black, red, and yellow painted tin van, decorated with gold stenciling; set on four iron wheels, with curved roof supported by three tin strips on each side of van, tailgate on rotating hinge; stenciled in gold "FANCY GOODS," with depiction of horse's head on side flaps; connected by triple rod curved harness on rotating hinge to two trotting horses (molded tin halves soldered together) attached across middle rod by band of tin and each attached at one forehoof to small articulated balancing wheel on axle.

5-11 "Kibbe's Confectionery" Wagon
Maker undetermined
U.S.A., c. 1850-1900
19" x 5" x 8"

Blue painted tin wagon, stenciled on both sides "KIBBE'S CONFECTION-ERY," with mudguard, quarter-rotating hood, red hollow trunk and hollow base with opening top; set on four iron wheels; connected by steel shaft to two horses (molded halves soldered together), each set on balancing wheel.

5-12 Open Wagon with Roof
Maker undetermined
U.S.A., c. 1850-1900
9" x 3" x 4¾"

Tin open wagon, painted blue, yellow, and red, with three posts on each side supporting roof, gingerbread trim on three sides; set on four iron wheels; connected by double rod harness to trotting white horse (molded halves soldered together).

5-13 "Yankee Notions" Peddling Wagon
Maker undetermined
U.S.A., c. 1850-1900
10½" x 3" x 4¾"

Tin peddling wagon, stenciled in black "YANKEE NOTIONS," painted red and black, with quarter-rotating hood, high mudguard, hollow trunk and hollow wagon base, both with opening tops; set on four cast-iron wheels; connected by triple rod harness to two horses (molded tin halves soldered together).

5-14 Water Truck with Driver and Horse
Maker undetermined
Germany or France,
c. 1880-1900
11½" x 3" x 6¼"

Tin water truck, consisting of brown barrel with orange funnel and lead faucet; set on orange chassis with four gilded tin wheels on steel axles; seated driver (molded tin halves clasped together), dressed in blue and orange with black top hat; truck connected by curved steel shafts to trotting white horse (similarly constructed). Eccentric rod from shaft to front axle causes horse to trot up and down when toy is pulled.

5-15 "G.A. Schwarz Toys Fancy Goods" Peddling Van
Maker undetermined
U.S.A., c. 1880
21½" x 6¾" x 10½"

Tin van, painted olive-green, red and pink, and decorated with gold stenciling; set on four iron wheels, with curved roof supported by three tin strips on each side of van. Two tin side flaps opening upwards on rotating hinges. Stenciled in gold "G.A. SCHWARZ TOYS FANCY GOODS. 1006 CHESTNUT ST. PHILA PA."; connected by curved rod harness on rotating hinge to two horses (molded tin halves clasped together), attached together by band of tin and each soldered by two hooves to small platform set on two small articulated balancing wheels.

5-16 "IXL Express Co." Wagon
James Fallows & Co.
Philadelphia, PA, c. 1895
21" x 5¼" x 8¼"

Blue and white painted tin express wagon, labeled in gold stencil on both sides "IXL EXPRESS CO.," with orange driver's seat and blue step; set on four iron wheels; with detachable driver (flat tin halves soldered together); connected by double rod harness to trotting brown horse (similarly constructed).

5-17 "Delivery Van"
Maker undetermined
Germany, c. 1900
9½" x 3" x 4¾"

Red, black and gilt delivery van, labeled "DELIVERY VAN" and "MADE IN GERMANY," with four wheels, front wheels smaller and pivoting; attached by shafts to trotting horse (molded tin halves clasped together). Steel barrel and spring mechanism beneath van.

6 | Horse-Drawn Wagons and Carts, Cast Iron

By the 1880s and 1890s cast-iron pull toys came to the forefront, although tin ones continued to be made in great quantity as well. The cast-iron toys were made by an entirely different technique, requiring more sophisticated operations and, in general, larger plants. The toys were made by pouring molten iron into molds consisting of wet sand (contained in a frame) into which designs had been impressed.

Typically a toy was cast in several parts and the parts then assembled by iron pins, bolts, and rivets. The sand-casting method allowed for almost infinite three-dimensional effects and for raised detailing. The relative importance of paint as detail declined, though most of the toys were painted and the molded detailing did allow for fancy highlighting in paint.

Cast-iron wagons and carts were made by all of the companies in the cast-iron toy business including Carpenter, Ives, Harris, Kenton, Hubley, and Dent, among others. They followed the patterns of the tin wagons and carts to a certain extent, but soon their toys took on an individuality of their own and usually featured horses which moved up and down (through one mechanical device or another) when the toy is pulled. Realistic cast-iron horses, drivers, and riders usually accompanied them, adding to their realism. Detachable harnesses, chains, and other accessories often appear on these toys also.

In addition to their three-dimensional realism, the cast-iron toys had another distinct advantage over their tin counterparts: durability. They are iron, after all, and they wear like it. On the other hand, they were relatively expensive and tin toys still served much of the market.

NOTE: Cast-iron toys are notoriously easy to fake. An impression is made in a sand mold using another cast-iron toy as a pattern; molten iron is then poured in—and the rest is obvious. There are ways to tell many faked items, however: first, the toy will be ever-so-slightly smaller than it should be due to shrinkage of the iron ("oversize" patterns were used by the toy companies to solve this problem; when a mold became unusable, another was made from the original pattern which was reserved for that purpose); details will likely be blurred and the surface rougher and grainier than on genuine specimens, the pieces will tend not to fit well, and the paint, even though it may appear "aged" will not have the proper patina.

6-0 "City Delivery" Van (color plate, left)
Harris Toy Co.
Toledo, OH, c. 1903
L. 15"

Cast-iron van with orange paneled base, yellow and green sides, black roof, two cut windows, labeled "City Delivery," with pivoting front chassis and movable tailgate, set on four yellow wheels. Nickel-plated cast-iron driver in suit and derby. Black iron workhorses set on two balancing wheels connected by rods and chains to van shaft. Horses move up and down when toy is pulled.

Donkey-Drawn Plantation Wagon (color plate, right)
Harris Toy Co.
Toledo, OH, c. 1903
L. 16½"

Blue plantation wagon and pivoting front chassis on four yellow wheels; tin bottom, red and blue cast-iron fenced sides. Iron donkeys with gilt bridles. Black barefoot driver in black clothes and white hat.

6-1 Cart
Ives, Blakeslee & Co.
Bridgeport, CT, c. 1880-1900
L. 9"

Red cart connected by black rod shafts to single black walking horse. Wires attached to two balancing wheels cause horse's legs to move alternately. Flat iron driver in working clothes.

6-2 Oxen Wagon
Dent Hardware Co.
Fullerton, PA, c. 1890
L. 15½"

Orange wagon with pivoting front chassis, yellow wheels, side steps. Pair of gilt oxen set on two balancing wheels and connected to chassis by elaborate shaft.

6-3 Stake Dump Cart Pulled by Donkey
Probably Walker and Crosby
Brooklyn, NY, c. 1890
L. 10"

Green cart with four stake sides and hinged tailgate, semi-rotating on axle set on two large red wheels. Cart dumps when manually unhooked from shafts. Donkey, with gilding, attached by rods and chains to shafts, on balancing wheels. Labeled "GSC" with half-moon design and "PAT. APL.24. '83 NOV. 10. '85" impressed on bottom.

6-4 Dump Cart
Francis W. Carpenter
Port Chester, NY, c. 1892
L. 12¾"

Red dump cart with removable bench decorated with black striping, semi-rotating on axle of two large black wheels, connected to shaft-frame assembly set on two balancing wheels. Trotting horse with rotating bit. Driver and passenger. Protrusion on balancing wheel causes horse to "trot" by lifting and releasing back leg. Star insignia and "PAT. MAY 25, 1880 REISS'D MAR. 14, 1882 PAT. NOV. 21 '82 & MAY 13 '84" (on cart), "PAT. NOV. 21 '82 & MAR 20 '83" (on chassis), "PAT. DEC. 20 '81" (on bench) and "PAT. NOV. 16 '80 PAT. JULY 19 '81" (on horse), all in relief.

6-5 Sprinkling Wagon
Wilkins Toy Co.
Keene, NH, c. 1895
L. 16½"

Orange tank wagon and pivoting chassis with black ribbing, brass capped hole in top and rubber-piped hole and sprinkler frame in lower rear, set on yellow wheels with orange striping. Pair of walking workhorses on balancing wheels with chain braces and singletrees.

6-6 Long "Dray"
Hubley Mfg. Co.
Lancaster, PA, c. 1900-10
L. 22½"

Green steel dray with black iron fenced sides and chains, pivoting front chassis, four large red wheels with gilt hubs and simulated nails. Pair of walking workhorses with leather reins, steel wire connecting braces. Black cast-iron driver in conical cap. Labeled "DRAY" in gilt relief.

6-7 "Pure Lake Ice" Wagon
Harris Toy Company
Toledo, OH, c. 1903
L. 13¼"

Orange cast iron van labeled "Pure Lake Ice" in gilt relief, with pivoting front chassis, brown roof, and open back, set on four yellow wheels. Pair of iron walking workhorses, on two balancing wheels connected to van shaft by chains and rods. Blue cast-iron driver in porter's uniform.

6-8 Oxen-Drawn Log Wagon
Hubley Mfg. Co.
Lancaster, PA, c. 1906
L. 15½"

Green oversized log with bark decoration attached to two yellow chassis, front and back, with heavy red wheels, pulled through means of shaft by pair of cast-iron oxen, with gilt horns, set on two balancing wheels. Black barefoot driver with rolled trousers and hat.

6-9 "Police Patrol" Wagon
Possibly Kenton Hardware Mfg.
Co.
Kenton, OH, c. 1911
L. 19¼"

Blue cast-iron wagon with pivoting front chassis, tin floor, gilt head-lamps and railings, set on concave orange wheels. Pair of galloping horses with connecting string braces on balancing wheel. Iron tab on axle rings bell under front chassis. Driver, three policemen, and "culprit," all cast iron.

6-10 No. "48 Express" Wagon
with Driver
Kenton Hardware Mfg. Co.
Kenton, OH, c. 1920
L. 16½"

Green gilt-trimmed cast-iron wagon with pivoting front chassis, gilt railings, set on four yellow wheels. Pair of galloping cast-iron horses set on two balancing wheels, connected by chain braces on steel plates to wagon shaft. Labeled "48" in relief and "Express" in gilt relief.

7 | Horse-Drawn Coaches and Carriages, Tin

It is in the area of coaches and carriages that the foreign tin-toy manufacturers excelled. Typically the tin chassis of a well-made German carriage is intricately folded, molded, and creased, its joints neatly soldered; details are made of hand-molded tin, lead, or iron; paint is applied by hand with a great deal of precision and flair; and the whole is set on an intricate suspension.

American carriages tend to show their development from the more primitive forms and rely heavily on stenciling for detail and have simpler design conceptions overall. This is not to say that there are not magnificent American tin carriages (7-6) and inferior German ones. The general point, however, is valid. (And if one needs consolation, even David Pressland agrees that the American tin horses which pull the carriages are superior in both overall design and lifelike feeling.)

These toy carriages and coaches came in as many forms as the real ones—landaus, phaetons, gigs, cabriolets, and on and on and on. In general, the fancier, larger, and better executed they are, the more desirable they are. The European handcrafted and hand-painted method was more costly at the time that the toys were made and, except for an American coach of great rarity, the European coaches command the greater price on the world market. Also, American tin toys of this sort tend to be more prevalent since they were cheaper to make and dominated the mass market when they were made.

Europeans did not adopt the American approach, but continued to turn out the "carriage trade" carriages until the end of the century. Then the Europeans, particularly the Germans, literally flooded the market with cheap, mass-produced lithographed tin toys (7-12).

7-0 Carriage on Fancy Chassis (color plate)
Maker undetermined
Germany, c. 1880
17½" x 5¼" x 7"

Tin carriage, painted russet and blue, with folded black hood and fenders attached to steps; set on elaborate yellow chassis with four slightly concave yellow wheels, front wheels on pivot joint; seated detachable cast-iron driver; attached by leather reins and harnesses to two trotting horses (intricate molded halves soldered together), soldered to flat yellow platforms each set on four small wheels. Horses' platforms kept rolling in unison by T-shaped tin harness attached to carriage chassis by revolving joint at one end and to front of horses by two chains at other end.

7-1 Blue Landau
Maker undetermined
U.S.A., c. 1850-1900
15¾" x 4" x 5¾" (carriage only)

Blue painted tin landau, with red roof, projecting rear guard, projecting buggy-style front seat with mudguard, and working hinged doors; set on red steel-rod chassis with four iron wheels, back wheels larger; seated driver (flat halves soldered together); attached by steel-rod shafts to white trotting horse (similarly constructed) with two legs set on tin stand on iron balancing wheel.

7-2 Gig
Maker undetermined
U.S.A., c. 1850-1900
12" x 2¾" x 4¼"

Painted tin orange and blue gig, without seat, with impressed ornate trim; set on two iron wheels; connected by double rod harness to trotting yellow horse (molded halves clasped together).

7-3 Carriage-Chariot
Maker undetermined
U.S.A., c. 1850-1900
11" x 3" x 3"

Tin carriage-chariot, gilded and painted orange and yellow, with two bucket seats and impressed leafy scrollwork sides, decorated with black pseudo-stenciling; set on four black iron wheels; connected by double rod harness to trotting horse (molded halves soldered together).

7-4 Cabriolet
Maker undetermined
U.S.A., c. 1850-1900
7" x 1¾" x 3½"

Orange painted tin cabriolet, with gilt stenciling, on two black iron wheels, with high curved mudguard and open back; connected by steel shafts to trotting horses (molded halves soldered together), with two feet resting on curved supporting rod.

7-5 Surrey
Maker undetermined
U.S.A., c. 1850-1900
7½" x 4½" x 6½" (carriage only)

Painted and stenciled tin surrey, blue, green, and red, with roof held up by two posts and two rods on each side, and with flat bottom set on four iron wheels; connected by detachable curved rod harness to two trotting white horses (molded halves soldered together), connected by band of tin.

7-6 Omnibus Carriage
Hull and Stafford
Clinton, CT, c. 1865
15½" x 4½" x 9"

Tin omnibus carriage, painted green, white, and red, with floral design and leaf-and-shell tin trim, three windows and draped curtains on each side, back step, open door and driver's step; set on four yellow cast-iron wheels, front wheels on pivot joint; seated driver, dressed in red tunic and black bowler; connected by triple rod harness to two trotting horses (molded tin halves soldered together), each soldered to curved rod support.

7-7 Phaeton
Maker undetermined
Possibly England, c. 1880
14½" x 3½" x 4½"

Green painted tin phaeton, with two red seats, mudguard, and folded top; set on four pink lead wheels; driver, dressed as jockey; connected by shafts to trotting white horse (molded halves soldered together). Embossed with crown on sides of phaeton.

7-8 Black Brougham Cab
Maker undetermined
Probably U.S.A., c. 1890
10" x 3½" x 8"

Black painted tin cabriolet, with delicate geometric yellow stenciling, open front with flat step, driver's seat at back on top of trunk; set on four yellow wheels with rubber tires; large clockwork in trunk.

7-9 Gig with Bouncing Driver
Maker undetermined
Possibly France, c. 1890
7¼" x 2½" x 5"

Red and blue painted tin gig, folded construction; set on two red iron wheels with tab on axle which moves rod connected to molded-tin driver; trotting horse (molded tin halves soldered together) set on balancing wheel. Driver bounces up and down on seat when toy is pulled.

7-10 Cabriolet
Maker undetermined
Germany, c. 1890-1910
7" x 2" x 4½" (carriage only)

Blue lithographed and gilded tin carbriolet, with white-highlighted window and lamp on each side; half-figure driver (tin halves clasped together); attached by two black steel shafts to lithographed tin horse (torso and head composed of clasped molded halves, flat-cut jointed legs); steel clockwork beneath back of cab. Cab rolls forward and horse's legs move when clockwork is activated.

7-11 Red Buggy with Jockey
Ives, Blakeslee and Williams Co.
Bridgeport, CT, c. 1893
12" x 3¼" x 6"

Red painted tin buggy, decorated with black striping, with green interior, yellow seat and high red mudguard; set on four black iron wheels, back wheels pivoting; seated jockey (molded tin halves soldered together); connected by red shaft to two galloping black horses (molded tin halves soldered together), horses attached by rods to axle running through brass and steel clockwork beneath buggy. Buggy rolls forward and horses gallop up and down when clockwork is activated.

7-12 Open Air Car
S. Gunthermann
Nuremberg, Germany, c. 1910
13" x 3¾" x 7"

Painted and lithographed tin open-air car, red and yellow, with seat and trunk, front lamps; set on four wheels with rubber tires; driver, wearing trousers, sporting jacket, and top hat; carriage and driver connected by double rod harness and rope reins to galloping brown horse (detailed molded halves clasped together); steel clockwork under trunk. Horse sways up and down and car moves forward when clockwork is activated. (This toy is also found in automobile version.) Labeled "ASGW."

8 | Horse-Drawn Coaches and Carriages, Cast Iron

Here, as in all areas of cast-iron toy manufacture, America was king. There was simply no competition from abroad. For whatever reason, with almost no exceptions, Europeans did not make cast-iron toys.

Some of the American coaches and carriages took extremely elaborate forms. The four-seater Hubley brake (color plate 8), the Carpenter tally-ho, the Wilkins landau, and the Dent phaeton (8-3, 8-4, 8-9) are all fancy forms of transportation indeed. And they are constructed in an elaborate manner, each with many castings, carefully molded, detailed, and painted, with life-like galloping horses and lively passengers.

But no matter how elegant these toys are, they do not take themselves quite so seriously as the prestigious European tin coaches. They are almost caricatures, perhaps poking a bit of fun at high-brows. The American makers do not seem quite at home with the coach and carriage forms.

The detailing on these toys is remarkable and should be noted by the collector, for some versions of these toys are likely to come on the market with parts missing or interchanged. The horses and the passengers are the most likely candidates, unless the model features detachable headlights and the like, which are often lost. Reins, chain braces, balancing wheels, and other separate parts are also often missing. A complete toy is a joy to find, but unfortunately not an everyday occurrence.

The collector should judge whether the toy is complete and correct in its details and, if not, what this should mean to him in terms of price and in terms of whether he should acquire it at all. Each collector will develop his own rules of thumb to fit his style of collecting.

8-0 Four-Seater Brake (color plate)
Hubley Mfg. Company
Lancaster, PA, c. 1920
L. 27½"

Black cast-iron brake, pivoting front chassis, with yellow grids and trim and black, yellow, and orange headlamps, bucket seat for driver, tin floor, on yellow wheels with black striping. Double-span horse tandem, galloping, set on four balancing wheels, connected by rods and brass beams, tin singletrees and crossbars. Driver with lap blanket, three male and two female passengers, and two liverymen, all with movable arms.

8-1 Double Surrey
Pratt & Letchworth
Buffalo, NY, c. 1892
L. 15¼"

Double cast-iron surrey with black steel base and pivoting front chassis on yellow wheels with orange stripes. Trotting horse set on small pivoting balancing wheels. Woman driver with movable arms.

8-2 Hansom Cab
Pratt & Letchworth
Buffalo, NY, c. 1892
L. 13"

Black hansom cab with yellow trim and red striping, high-backed driver's seat, square-cut windows and lamps on both sides, set on two black wheels with red striping. Galloping black horse. Liveried driver and woman passenger.

8-3 Tally-Ho Coach
Francis W. Carpenter
Port Chester, NY, c. 1895
L. 26¼"

Cream-white and black tally-ho coach, doors and lamps in relief, square-cut windows, projecting and suspended steps, four benches on roof, with pivoting front chassis, set on four red wheels, with crossbars, single-trees, and chain braces. Elaborate shaft mechanism to move horses, set on four balancing wheels. Two pairs of horses in tandem. Flat cast-iron liveried driver, passengers, and bugler with gilt bugle. Labeled "PAT. NOV. 16 '80 & MAR' 20 '83" in relief on shafts.

8-4 Landau
Wilkins Toy Co.
Keene, NH, c. 1895
L. 15"

Black landau, pivoting front chassis, with gilt trim and headlamps on either side, set on yellow wheels. Cut windows, opening doors. Pair of galloping horses. Liveried driver and attendant.

8-5 Road Cart
Wilkins Toy Co.
Keene, NY, c. 1895
L. 10¼"

Yellow road cart with simulated upholstered seat, fenced arm rests, mud guard, set on two large orange wheels. Rearing horse, connected to cart by orange shafts, set on balancing wheel. Woman driver, in elaborate dress holding string reins.

8-6 Buckboard Pulled by Goats
Probably Harris Toy Company
Toledo, OH, c. 1903
L. 13½"

Yellow-planked buckboard set on two slightly concave red wheels with perforated bench, pulled by pair of trotting goats (moved by shaft-brace-crossbar mechanism) connected to pivoting front chassis and set on two balancing wheels. Woman driver.

8-7 Dog Cart with Jockey
Harris Toy Co.
Toledo, OH, c. 1903
L. 10"

Black fancy gig, with simulated upholstery, gilt armrests, and mud-guard, set on two yellow wheels, pulled by trotting dog, attached by shaft, set on balancing wheel. Driver dressed in jockey's uniform.

8-8 Surrey
Possibly Hubley Mfg. Co.
Lancaster, PA, c. 1906
L. 13"

Yellow surrey with steel body and iron pivoting front chassis, set on orange iron steel wheels. Galloping cast-iron horse on immobile balancing wheels. Woman passenger on steel bench and liveried driver, both of cast iron.

8-9 Black Spider Phaeton
Possibly Dent Hardware Co.
Fullerton, PA, c. 1910
L. 13½"

Black phaeton, pivoting front chassis, with gilt trim and gilt lamps in relief on either side of folded hood; set on two yellow wheels. Galloping horse on balancing wheel. Driver, liveryman and passenger.

8-10 Cabriolet
Kenton Hardware Mfg. Co.
Kenton, OH, c. 1911
L. 14½"

Black cabriolet, pivoting front chassis, with green and gilt trim and circular cut windows on either side of hood; set on two large slightly concave yellow wheels. Pair of galloping black horses, set off-center by rods on two balancing wheels. Driver with movable arms and woman passenger. Horses gallop up and down when toy is pulled.

9 | Horse-Drawn Fire Equipment, Tin

Tin horse-drawn fire equipment is rare. When it can be found, it is often in relatively poor condition, and it is expensive.

The first tin toys of this type appear to have been made around 1860 in Connecticut, notably by George W. Brown & Co. Other companies also made similar toys, often with clockwork components, including James Fallows & Co. of Philadelphia and Althof, Bergmann & Co. of New York. Examples from all three companies are illustrated.

In many ways, early tin fire engines are similar to early tin trains (see section 26). Though they may be based on actual prototypes, their features tend to be exaggerated and they have a fanciful rather than realistic appearance, with exaggerated chimneys and cylinders and bright stylized decorations, often in fancy geometric and floral patterns with imaginative stenciled names. The true fire engine, or pumper, is the most commonly found form.

The graceful painted tin horses which pull the equipment are attached in various ways, usually by steel rods or strips, in a rather crude and unrealistic manner. The simple and naïve tin fire equipment is to be compared with the comparatively complex and sophisticated cast-iron fire equipment which replaced it and which took realism in toys to new heights.

9-0 "Neptune" Fire Engine (color plate)
Possibly James Fallows & Co.
Philadelphia, PA, c. 1870-90
14½" x 4¼" x 8"

Painted tin fire engine, with black cylindrical base stenciled in gilt "NEPTUNE," orange boiler with gilt stenciled trim, orange chimney with gilt pie-plate cover, black steam chest with pie-plate cover on base;

set on four iron wheels; driver (molded tin halves soldered together); engine attached by shafts to pair of trotting white horses (similarly constructed), connected to one another by steel band; brass and steel clockwork beneath boiler.

9-1 Fire Engine on Platform with Projecting Front Wheels
Possibly George W. Brown and Co.
Forestville, CT, c. 1860
10" x 5¼" x 7¾"

Painted tin fire engine, with red boiler and black covered chimney set at center of yellow platform wagon, decorated with black-stenciled trim; wagon with pipe-like black vertical steam ejector behind boiler and with large gilt cylinders topped with tube-like black cylinders on each side; set on two red iron back wheels and on a pair of projecting red iron front wheels which pivot on steel-rod brace; iron bell beneath one cylinder; steel and brass clockwork inset in bottom. (Horses missing.)

9-2 Hose Carriage
George W. Brown and Co.
Forestville, CT, c. 1860
13" x 5½" x 10"

Tin hose carriage, painted red and white, with blue and red stenciling and floral plaque on each side, barrel revolving on steel rod axis; chassis, horizontal cylinder at each end; set on four large cast iron wheels. (Horses missing.)

9-3 Fire Engine
Maker undetermined
U.S.A., c. 1870-1900
17" x 3" x 7¾"

Painted tin fire engine, with black cylindrical base, red boiler and smokestack and high driver's seat; set on four steel wheels; bell soldered beneath boiler and clapper attached to bend in front axle; seated driver (molded tin halves clasped together) dressed in blue and white with black top hat; engine connected by shafts to trotting horse (similarly constructed); set on platform with small balancing wheel.

9-4 Fire Engine with Gingerbread Trim
Possibly Althof, Bergmann and Co.
New York, NY, c. 1880
11" x 4¾" x 9¼" (engine only)

Painted tin fire engine, with blue and black tin cylindrical base, vertical red- and black-striped boiler with gingerbread trim and black smokestack, curved steel pistons, yellow cylindrical pump, brown folded burlap steam ejector with brass finial; set on four iron wheels; seated molded tin fireman driver and brakeman; pulled by pair of galloping brown horses (molded tin halves soldered together), soldered to bent rod shafts, attached to one another by tin strip, and set on second tin strip on two small iron balancing wheels.

9-5 "Union" Fire Engine
Possibly James Fallows and Sons
Philadelphia, PA, c. 1883
12" x 3" x 6"

Painted tin fire engine, with black cylindrical base stenciled in gilt "UNION," orange boiler with gilt roof stenciled with shield, bell on bottom; set on four iron wheels; driver in blue uniform at front; connected by shafts to trotting horse (molded halves soldered together). Stenciled "PAT JUNE 5 '83."

10 Horse-Drawn Fire Equipment, Pumpers, Cast Iron

Cast-iron horse-drawn fire equipment (sections 10-13) has been for many years one of the most popular areas of American toy manufacturers and toy collectors alike.

The common source of original attraction was the real fire engines of the last quarter of the nineteenth century and the early years of the twentieth—magnificently conceived and executed specimens with gleaming brass and mirror-like paint, intricately detailed in accessories and trim, pulled by prize horses, all often the pride and joy of a community or neighborhood. The toys which were inspired by these machines were hardly less elaborate and were made without interruption from the 1870s until 1930 or so—and then again by at least one company (Kenton) from 1939 through 1954.

The pumper (called simply "fire engine" by purists) was the most common form made. As its name implies, this was the machine which created the pressure necessary to force water through fire hoses onto the fire. In real life it was the mechanical center of attention at a fire—the piece of equipment which made the noise, gave off the steam, and so forth, and as such, it seems to have captured the imagination of the toy manufacturers.

The typical example has representations of the boiler, pumps, steam ejector, pistons, cylinders and all the rest of this then-complex equipment, arranged in various ways on various models, and is painted with bright colors and often trimmed with gilt and hand striping.

As with other fire equipment, the horses are usually specialized "fire horses," which are depicted in cast iron as sleek but strong specimens in a life-like galloping pose and often move up and down realistically as the toy is pulled, activated by various types of mechanisms. Also, the firemen are lifelike and brightly uniformed, usually detachable from the fire equipment.

10-0 Pumper (color plate)
Pratt & Letchworth
Buffalo, NY, c. 1892
L. 17"

Black and green pumper with gilt trim, gilt steam ejector, gilt-trimmed nickel-plated pistons and pumps, boiler and immobile balancing wheels. Pivoting front chassis. Orange wheels with black striping. Two galloping detachable horses, fitted to shaft prongs and tin crossbar, with pivoting singletrees. Bell under chassis rung by axle tab.

10-1 Pumper
Francis W. Carpenter
Port Chester, NY, c. 1880-1900

Cast-iron pumper fire engine with gilt trim, gilt steam ejector, black piston and pump, gray cast-iron and unpainted steel boiler, set on orange wheels (front wheels pivot). Two galloping horses connected to fire engine by chain braces and shaft and set on two notched balancing wheels, with prongs which cause horses to move up and down. Labeled in relief "53."

10-2 Pumper with Eagle
Ives, Blakeslee and Williams Co.
Bridgeport, CT, c. 1893
L. 18¾"

Gilt-trimmed black fire engine, with pivoting front chassis, wooden steam ejector with gilt lead eagle on top, and rotating balancing wheels; set on two slightly concave wheels. Pair of Ives "Type II" galloping horses connected to one another by chain and to brass brace by spring rod. Shaft labeled "PHOENIX" in relief.

10-3 Black and Gilt Pumper
Possibly Kenton Hardware Co.
Kenton, OH, c. 1900
L. 14½"

Black fire engine, on pivoting front chassis, with gilt trim and gilt steam ejector, balancing wheels and undetachable fireman driver. Galloping three-horse span, with chain braces; outside horses attached off-center by rods to two balancing wheels which cause them to gallop when toy is pulled.

10-4 Pumper with Stationary Horses
Probably Harris Toy Co.
Toledo, OH, c. 1903
L. 17"

Black, gilt-trimmed pumper with steam ejector, piston pump, boiler with detailed meters, and red pivoting front chassis, set on yellow wheels with simulated nails. Stationary horses attached to red iron shaft.

10-5 Pumper with Tandem Horse Team
Probably Dent Hardware Co.
Fullerton, PA, c. 1905
L. 36"

Cream-colored pumper with gilded "diamond" trim set on red and silver wheels with gilt striping, pivoting front chassis. Cast-iron center shaft between two pairs of horses, variously colored. Shaft and crossbar mechanism cause horses to gallop alternately and steel bell to ring. Gilt steam ejector, twin pistons and pumps, boiler with gilt gauges, revolving blue balancing wheels, lead lantern with mica cover, gilt lead eagle ornament.

10-6 Nickel-Plated Pumper
Possibly Hubley Mfg. Co.
Lancaster, PA, c. 1910 (?)
L. 21"

Nickel-plated fire engine, with pivoting front chassis, steam ejector, piston, pump, boiler, and rotating balancing wheels; set on two large, slightly concave orange wheels. Pair of galloping horses set on balancing wheel.

10-7 Copper-Plated Pumper
Probably Kenton Hardware Mfg. Co.
Kenton, OH, c. 1911
L. 16"

Copper-plated pumper with steam ejector, twin pistons, boiler and rotating balancing wheels, with pivoted front chassis, on four wheels. Pair of galloping copper-plated horses with gilt chain braces. Steel bell beneath chassis.

10-8 Nickel-Plated Pumper
Possibly Kenton Hardware Mfg. Co.
Kenton, OH, c. 1911
L. 19"

Nickel-plated fire engine, with boiler, pistons, revolving red balancing wheels, bronze steam ejector; set on wheels with simulated nails. Galloping three-horse span, connected to one another by steel rod through shafts set on iron balancing wheels and pulling crossbar. Driver and fireman in blue uniforms with flat red hats.

10-9 Nickel Plated and Painted Pumper
Hubley Mfg. Co.
Lancaster, PA, c. 1920
L. 21½"

Orange and gilt-trimmed pumper, pivoting front chassis, with nickel-plated parts including steam ejector, pistons, and pumps; boiler with detailed gauges and hose hooks. Two horses, one nickel-plated and one painted, moving on shaft prongs and set on balancing wheels, connected to crossbar with chain braces. Steel bell under chassis struck by lead tab on front wheel axle.

11 | Horse-Drawn Fire Equipment, Hose Carriages, Cast Iron

The cast-iron toy hose carriage does not have the mechanical excitement of the pumper, but it does have an obvious feature which made it a rival for popularity—the hose reel (or wheel) which revolved on an axle to unwind a length of hose (usually made of rubber or woven cotton) with a metal or wooden nozzle. This type of feature, which involved the child in a simulation of real-life action, was to be modified and expanded upon over the years in countless other toys.

Needless to say, each of the cast-iron toy companies had its line of fire equipment, often its best seller. The early years are dominated by Ives, Carpenter, and Pratt & Letchworth; Hubley and Kenton made the most extensive lines in the 1920s and 1930s. During the intervening years, many more companies, including Dent and Wilkins, were producing these toys.

As usual, the earlier toys are more desirable, not only for their comparative rarity, but for their superior workmanship and design. By the post-World War I period, the toys become over-simplified in design, with fewer detailed parts and paint less carefully applied.

11-0 Hose Carriage (color plate)
Pratt and Letchworth
Buffalo, NY, c. 1892
L. 14"

Black and green cast-iron carriage with gilt trim, rotating green and orange hose reel with white rubber hose, set on two large orange wheels with black striping. Iron knob on axle rings gilt steel bell. Galloping horse set off-center on small balancing wheel.

11-1 Two-Wheeled Hose Carriage
Maker undetermined
American, c. 1880-1920
L. 12"

Black cast-iron hose carriage with gilt and orange trim, orange immobile hose reel with wooden axle-barrel, set on two large orange wheels. Trotting black horse set on treaded balancing wheel. Driver has movable arms and horse moves when pulled.

11-2 Orange and Maroon Hose Carriage
Maker undetermined
U.S.A., c. 1880-1920
L. 16"

Orange hose carriage, with pivoting front chassis; set on two large wheels with simulated nails; detachable rotating hose reel; galloping horse, set on balancing wheel and attached to shafts.

11-3 Two-Wheeled Hose Carriage
Francis W. Carpenter
Port Chester, NY, c. 1892
L. 14½"

Black stenciled hose carriage, rotating hose reel with one-piece fluid-designed chassis extending into shafts. Treaded dual wheels with prong mechanism causes horse to trot when toy is pulled. Labeled in relief "PAT NOV. 21 '82 OCT. 23 '83 MAY 13 '84" on carriage and "PAT. NOV. 16 '80 PAT. JULY 19 '81" on horse.

11-4 Hose Carriage
Ives, Blakeslee and Williams Co.
Bridgeport, CT, c. 1893
L. 15"

Black and orange carriage with gilt trim, black and gilt rotating hose reel with sunburst pattern, set on two large orange wheels; Ives "Type II" galloping horse, which moves up and down when toy is pulled.

11-5 Orange and Green Hose Carriage
Possibly Hubley Mfg. Co.
Lancaster, PA, c. 1900
L. 16"

Green cast-iron hose carriage, with pivoting front chassis, impressed "462," with gilt trim; set on four slightly concave orange wheels. Orange cast-iron hose reel, rotating, with wooden axle-barrel and gilt trim. Nickel-plated cast-iron trotting horse; set on balancing wheel and connected to shafts.

11-6 Hose Carriage
Dent Hardware Co.
Fullerton, PA, c. 1905
L. 14½"

Mustard-colored cast-iron hose carriage with rotating hose-reel decorated in ornate gilt relief; red and silver iron wheels. Black and white horses gallop and bell rings when toy is pulled.

11-7 Copper-Plated Hose
Carriage
Kenton Hardware Mfg. Co.
Kenton, OH, c. 1911
L. 14"

Copper-plated cast-iron hose carriage and hose reel with rotating red wooden barrel cylinder and woven cotton hose, set on two large nickel-plated cast-iron wheels and also two nickel-plated wheels under pivoting front chassis; copper-plated galloping ho:ses with nickel-plated shaft, on two balancing wheels, connected to chassis by chain braces. Labeled in relief "Kenton."

11-8 No. "5 Hose" Wagon
Possibly Kenton Hardware Mfg.
Co.
Kenton, OH, c. 1911
L. 18"

Red wagon, with pivoting front chassis, gilt railings, gilt chemical tanks and underslung cage; set on four red and silver wheels. Pair of galloping horses, attached to chain braces suspended from cross bar. Labeled in gilt relief "5 HOSE."

11-9 Hose Carriage with Nickel-Plated Hose Reel
Kenton Hardware Mfg. Co.
Kenton, OH, c. 1911
L. 13"

Orange hose carriage, with pivoting front chassis, undetachable fireman driver in blue coat and silver helmet; set on four large yellow wheels. Nickel-plated hose reel, with ornate decorations. Pair of galloping horses; set on two immobile balancing wheels and attached to yellow shaft. Labeled in relief "KENTON BRAND."

11-10 Copper-Plated Hose Carriage
Kenton Hardware Mfg. Co.
Kenton, OH, c. 1911
L. 14"

Copper-plated hose carriage, with pivoting front chassis; hose reel with rotating red wooden barrel-cylinder and woven cotton hose; set on four nickel-plated cast-iron wheels. Pair of galloping copper-plated horses connected to one another by steel rod through nickel-plated shaft on two balancing wheels. Horses gallop up and down when toy is pulled. Labeled in relief "KENTON."

12 | Horse-Drawn Fire Equipment, Hook and Ladders, Cast Iron

The king of cast-iron horse-drawn fire equipment was the hook and ladder truck. It tended to be the largest in the general line of fire toys —and its construction tended to be the most complex, often incorporating tin and wood elements along with the basic cast iron.

The ladders which were featured on original equipment were sometimes wood and/or tin, not always cast iron, and tin was also often employed in the undercarriages of these toys. The whole, when brightly painted, however, has more often than not a convincing unity of design.

The more elaborate hook and ladder equipment also carried a variety of removable accessories including, besides ladders, hatchets, buckets, helmets and other fire-fighting paraphernalia. Naturally, it is desirable if one can acquire as many of the original accessories as possible, but this can rarely be done. When one does come upon a "complete" piece of equipment, caution should be used since replacements are difficult to detect; it is common to see accessories made by perhaps two or three different companies displayed on a hook and ladder made by still another company. Also, regrettably, completely phony accessories are sometimes offered for sale.

12-O Hook and Ladder (color plate)
Kenton Hardware Mfg. Co.
Kenton, OH, c. 1920
L. 30"

White hook and ladder carriage and yellow front chassis set on yellow wheels. Suspended under-carriage with tin floor and hooks for accessories. Steel bell rung by rod suspended beneath crossbar, struck by bent axle. Numerous accessories including iron helmets and hatchets.

12-1 Red Hook and Ladder
Francis W. Carpenter
Port Chester, NY, c. 1885-1900
L. 25½"

Red hook and ladder carriage and front chassis with underslung bar for accessories and braces for ladder. Pair of horses attached to singletrees by chain braces. Shaft from chassis with projecting prongs set on two balancing wheels. Horses trot as back legs are lifted and released by prongs when toy is pulled. Labeled in relief "PAT. MAY 13'84" and "PAT. NOV. 18(')80 MAR. 20'83: and on horses "PAT. NOV. 18'80 PAT. JULY 19'81."

12-2 Black Hook and Ladder
Possibly Ives, Blakeslee and Williams Co.
Bridgeport, CT, c. 1885-1900
L. 34½"

Black hook and ladder carriage and front chassis with cut-out decoration, underslung yellow beam for accessories and two suspended red ladders; set on concave wheels with simulated nails. Pair of galloping Ives "Type II" horses with chain braces.

12-3 Hook and Ladder
Pratt and Letchworth
Buffalo, NY, c. 1892
L. 26¼"

Black cast-iron hook and ladder carriage and pivoting front chassis with green and gilt trim set on orange wheels with black striping. Pair of galloping white horses set on tin balancing wheel, pivoting singletrees. Gilt brass bell stuck by lead tab attached to axle.

12-4 Hook and Ladder
Pratt and Letchworth
Buffalo, NY, c. 1892
L. 26¼"

Black hook and ladder carriage and front chassis with gilt and green trim; set on orange wheels with black striping. Pair of galloping horses partly rotating on horizontal rods and resting on off-center tin balancing wheel. Gilt brass bell with external lead clapper suspended beneath chassis. Horses gallop up and down and clapper strikes bell when toy is pulled.

12-5 Black Hook and Ladder
Ives, Blakeslee and Williams Co.
Bridgeport, CT, c. 1893
L. 28½"

Black hook and ladder, with gilt front and back seats and steering wheel, underslung hooked beam for accessories; set on two wheels. Pair of black Ives "Type II" galloping horses with molded details and chain braces, set off-center by rods on balancing wheel, connected to shaft labeled in relief "PHOENIX" pulling pivoting orange front chassis. Accessories and two firemen. Horses gallop when toy is pulled.

12-6 Hook and Ladder
Wilkins Toy Co.
Keene, NH, c. 1895
L. 26½"

Black and pastel-blue hook and ladder carriage and pivoting front chassis set on orange wheels. Pair of galloping white horses set on two pivoting balance wheels on bodies and two treaded balancing wheels at back feet. Movable cast-iron steering wheel. Two cast-iron ladders, one wooden ladder with steel rungs.

12-7 Hook and Ladder
Dent Hardware Co.
Fullerton, PA, c. 1900
L. 31"

White cast-iron hook and ladder

body and pivoting front chassis, ornate gilt floral trim, gilt head-lamps, bucket seat with rotating steering wheel in back, under-slung platform for accessories, set on red and gilt wheels. Galloping three-horse span on two balanc-ing wheels. Gilt steel bell under chassis. Three cast-iron ladders.

12-8 White and Red Hook and Ladder
Maker undetermined
Possibly Kenton Hardware Mfg. Co.
Kenton, OH, c. 1911
L. 19"

White gilt-trimmed hook and lad-der carriage and pivoting front chassis set on four red wheels. Span of three galloping horses, connected by chain braces to crossbars, on two balancing wheels.

12-9 Nickel-Plated "No. 126" Hook and Ladder
The Hubley Mfg. Co.
Lancaster, PA, c. 1920
L. 31½"

Nickel-plated hook and ladder with parallel ladder braces, hooks for accessories, orange iron back steering wheel, orange tin sus-pended carriage, set on two maroon and gilt iron wheels. Dec-orative "126" in pierced relief. Pulled by three galloping horses set on two balancing wheels. Bell and leather tab mechanism be-neath pivoting front chassis also on two maroon and gilt wheels. Leather reins, three cast-iron lad-ders, orange cast-iron hatchet, two nickel-plated buckets, with wire handles. Hook and ladder carriage impressed "462" and chassis impressed "110."

13 | Horse-Drawn Fire Equipment, Other, Cast Iron

In addition to the general line of fire equipment (pumpers, hose carriages, and hook and ladder equipment), the makers of cast-iron toys also produced certain specialty items, and these items are, on the whole, rarer and more costly than the foregoing.

Chemical wagons are generally rather elaborate productions, sometimes with a tank of brass or other shiny metal. In basic design, however, they tend to be similar to the equipment already discussed, with pivoting front chassis, galloping horses, and so forth. The fire patrol wagon (incomplete without its complement of "patrolling" fireman) is a dray-like affair with benches to seat the firemen. It is similar to the cast-iron police patrol wagon. The fire chief's wagon can also be quite elaborate, as is justifiable as the conveyance for the head of the fire company. Rarer than these three (all illustrated in color) is the fire tower (13-4) which in some versions actually sprayed water after being cranked or manually lifted upright from its wagon base. The fire pump (13-1) pumps water also and is rarer still.

Finally, the fire house with emerging pumper (13-3) should be singled out. It was possibly the most exciting cast-iron fire fighting toy produced.

13-0 "Chemical" Tank Wagon (color plate, top)
Maker undetermined
Possibly Kenton Hardware Mfg. Co.
Kenton, OH, c. 1880-1920
L. 22"

Yellow, red-trimmed wagon labelled "CHEMICAL" in relief on nickel-plated horizontal tank. Braces for ladders. Orange wheels. Span of three galloping horses, with chain braces, activated by shaft-and-rod mechanism and set on three balancing wheels. Bent axle strikes bell under crossbar.

"Fire Patrol" Wagon (color plate, center)
Pratt & Letchworth
Buffalo, NY, c. 1892
L. 16½"

Pastel blue wagon labeled "FIRE PATROL" in gilt. Gilt and wooden chemical tanks and pierced benches. Four blue and white wheels, front wheels pivoting. Two galloping horses with chain braces. Treaded balancing wheels with prongs cause horses to move. Four cast-iron firemen with moveable arms.

"Chief" Wagon (color plate, bottom)
Ives, Blakeslee and Williams Co.
Bridgeport, CT, c. 1893
L. 14¾"

Black wagon, with orange pivoting front chassis, labeled "CHIEF" in gilded relief; yellow trim and wheels. Ives "Type II" galloping horse, moved by bent axle mechanism.

**13-1 Fire Pump with Hose
Maker undetermined
Possibly George W. Brown and
     Co.
Forestville, CT, c. 1870
11½" x 5½" x 10½"**

Red cast-iron and tin working
hand pump; set on four elaborate
cast-iron wheels. Black rubber
hose with lead nozzle pumps
water when cast-iron handle is
pushed up and down.

**13-2 "Fire Patrol" Wagon
Ives, Blakeslee and Williams Co.
Bridgeport, CT, c. 1893
L. 20¾"**

Black wagon, labeled in gilt relief "FIRE PATROL," with gilt simulated
upholstered and perforated benches in back, gilt railings, and black
and gilt trunk with opening lid; set on concave orange wheels. Pulled
by pair of Ives "Type II" horses. Driver and six sitting cast-iron firemen in
brown and blue uniforms, each 3¼" high. Shaft labeled "PHOENIX" in
gilt relief.

**13-3 "Fire Engine House" with
     Fire Engine
Ives, Blakeslee and Williams Co.
Bridgeport, CT, c. 1893
15" x 8½" x 12"**

Building labeled in gilt relief "FIRE
ENGINE HOUSE," with shellacked
wooden walls, slanted roof and
floor, four cut windows with cast-
iron frames on each side, and
cast-iron façade with two opening cast-iron doors; clockwork
mechanism inside behind
opaque front windows; stop/start
hook at side. Black cast-iron fire
engine, with gilt steam ejector,
rotating balancing wheels, black
piston, black and gilt boiler; set on
yellow and black-striped wheels;
pulled by a pair of galloping
black cast-iron horses. From an
1893 Ives catalogue: "Wind as

you would a clock, pull out the stop wire at the side, and after the bell has struck one, two, one, two, three, the doors will fly open and the engine will start for the fire."

**13-4 Fire Water Tower Wagon
Maker undetermined
Possibly Wilkins Toy Co.
Keene, NH, c. 1900
L. 42¼"**

Water tower wagon set on steel dray frame pulled by animated three-horse span. Cast iron water tower featuring rotating frame and hollow tube along its length is manually raised for operation.

**13-5 "Chemical" Tank Wagon with Hose and Ladders
Possibly Dent Hardware Co.
Fullerton, PA, c. 1905
L. 22"**

Red cast-iron dray wagon labeled in gilt relief "CHEMICAL," featuring gilt tin chemical tank with gilt iron eagle; pulled by animated galloping three-horse span. Red and black cast-iron ladders on gilt pole-braces.

**13-6 "Chief" Wagon
Hubley Mfg. Co.
Lancaster, PA, c. 1910
L. 12½"**

Red wagon, labeled in gilt relief "CHIEF," with seat and open back; set on large red wheels; pulled by galloping black horse set on balancing wheel.

14 | Circus and Carnival Wagons

Though there are examples of nineteenth-century circus toys, their heyday did not come until the twentieth century. Even the later toys are quite desirable, however, and, in general, circus toys are the second most sought-after type of cast-iron toys (after horse-drawn fire equipment).

Horse-drawn cast-iron circus toys were generally manufactured in "parade" groups, including cage wagons with animals, band wagons, calliopes, chariots, and wagons with animated figures on their roofs. Assembling an entire matched set is quite an accomplishment if done piecemeal—and a good investment. The most extensive line of cast-iron circus toys is Hubley's "Royal Circus" (color plate 14, 14-5) which was made from 1910 to 1930.

The next most important line is the "Overland Circus" of the Kenton Hardware Mfg. Company (14-8), which was made from 1939 well into the 1950s—a curious revival of "old-fashioned" horse-drawn toys—and this is represented here because of its place in the tradition of the cast-iron horse-drawn pull toy, even though it falls outside the general date range of this book.

Also from time to time other types of toy circus wagons were made —tin, wooden, friction, and so forth (14-1), since the circus provided a "natural" in visual excitement which the toy maker could copy. But when a toy collector mentions circus toys, he usually means the Hubley and Kenton cast-iron varieties.

14-0 "Royal Circus" Cage Wagon with Giraffe (color plate)
Hubley Mfg. Co.
Lancaster, PA, c. 1920
L. 16½"

Cage wagon, with red cast-iron barred sides, red tin roof; set on yellow wheels with simulated nails; containing yellow cast-iron giraffe with head through hole in roof. Pulled by pair of white cast-iron horses with fancy harness and silver and red plumes. Labeled "ROYAL CIRCUS" in relief.

14-1 Cage Wagon with Elephants
Maker undetermined
U.S.A., c. 1850-1900
L. 11"

Tin cage wagon, painted red and green, barred on three sides, open at front, with slots for four tin animal figures on floor, and detachable roof; set on large cast-iron wheels. Pulled by tin elephants, with leader, all made of molded halves soldered together and fixed to green tin platform on wheels.

**14-2 Military Band Van
Morton Converse and Son
Winchendon, MA, c. 1900
L. 18½"**

Van, decorated on each side with yellow, orange, and black litho-graphed depiction of military brass band, with fan-bent tin seat and wooden base; set on orange wheels, front wheels on pivot joint. Pulled by two trotting tin horses (molded halves clasped together). Labeled on each side "CONVERSE" and "MADE IN U.S.A."

**14-3 Gilt Band Wagon with Driver
and Musicians
Possibly Hubley Mfg. Co.
Lancaster, PA, c. 1910
L. 30¾"**

Cast-iron band wagon and chassis, with gilt sides decorated with vines and horses' and lions' heads in relief, gilt back with de-sign depicting bareback rider; set on two large yellow cast-iron wheels; pulled by double-span tandem trotting silver and brown horse team; horses connected to each other by steel rods on springs set on off-center balanc-ing wheel and connected to crossbar by chain braces; steel suspended bell. Driver, four trum-peters and four horn players in red and black uniforms with bronze in-struments.

**14-4 Eagle Chariot with Woman
Driver
Kenton Hardware Mfg. Co.
Kenton, OH, c. 1911-20
L. 11½"**

Eagle-shaped chariot, cast-iron, silver and gilt paint, silver base decorated with blue stars; set on two red wheels; attached by crossbar, shaft, and chain braces to two galloping horses, set on two immobile balancing wheels. Standing woman driver with long hair and dressed in white robes.

14-5 "Royal Circus" Van with Acrobatic Clown
Hubley Mfg. Co.
Lancaster, PA, c. 1920
L. 15"

Van and pivoting chassis with blue cast-iron sides decorated with gilt angels in relief, oval aluminum mirror on each side, blue tin roof and front, footboard at front, two gilt and blue iron braces at top; set on four yellow cast-iron back wheels with simulated nails, pulled by pair of black cast-iron walking workhorses, with red and gilt iron plumes and molded detail. Cast-iron driver in red porter's uniform. Cast-iron clown with large white face on both sides of head, telescoped body with feet in red shoes and arms swinging on bar overhead. Clown swings between braces when toy is pulled.

14-6 Circus Calliope
Hubley Mfg. Co.
Lancaster, PA, c. 1920-30
L. 16"

Blue cast-iron calliope and chassis, with ornate gilt trim depicting angel trumpeters and organ pipes, with inside seat, driver's footboard, gilt boiler chimney; set on four red and gilt fanned wheels; pulled by a pair of walking brown horses, with molded gilt detail, set on two balancing wheels, attached to one another by rod through torsos. Driver and calliope player in red uniforms, 2½" high each. Impressed "11[5?]0."

14-7 "Big-Show Circus" Wagon
Ferdinand Strauss Corp.
New York, NY, c. 1930
L. 9"

Lithographed tin cage wagon, labeled "BIG-SHOW CIRCUS" and "93," blue with yellow, red, and green trim, clowns with drums, and driver in yellow uniform at wheel, containing flat-cut tin lion and tamer activated by barrel and spring mechanism. Labeled "THE FERDINAND STRAUSS CORP. NEW YORK U.S.A." and "STRAUSS MECHANICAL TOYS 'Known the World over'." Note: This is an automobile version of the traditional circus wagon form.

14-8 "Overland Circus" Cage Wagon with Polar Bear
Kenton Hardware Mfg. Co.
Kenton, OH, c. 1940-55
L. 14"

Red cast-iron cage wagon, with gilt trim and horizontally opening back door and set on two yellow wheels, containing polar bear. Pulled by pair of white trotting horses, set on two immobile balancing wheels, and pulling yellow shaft attached to pivoting front chassis on two yellow wheels. Driver and rider. Impressed "3314 MADE IN U.S.A. 3316" and labeled in relief "OVERLAND CIRCUS."

15 | See-Saws

In the foregoing sections it is demonstrated again and again that in the United States during the last century the ethic of work, a preference for realistic descriptions of everyday life, and a pervasive seriousness influenced the design of many toys. As we have seen in the previous section (circus toys) this was not always the case. Even in these exceptions, however, one still does not have the sense of childish play, romantic fantasy, and downright giddiness that one finds in certain of the foreign toys being made during the same time period.

The selection of see-saw toys here is illustrative. The Ives see-saw, shown in color, holds a pair of very prim and proper Victorian children, dressed in their Sunday best, tipping back and forth in a matter-of-fact, realistic manner. Contrast these with the German clowns (15-2) who are riding an improbable machine which never existed in reality—and rolling a ball back and forth between them to boot.

It seems to have been in the 1890s that German toys began to flood the world market, and one might venture to say that they were successful not only because they were cheap, but also, in the case of at least some of them, that they were more fun. This theme of European inventiveness and romance affected American competition and the results can be seen in some of the following toys.

15-0 Boy and Girl on Seesaw (color plate)
Ives, Blakeslee and Co.
Bridgeport, CT, c. 1870-90
18" x 2½" x 5½"

Painted wood seat and curved cone-shaped wood and tin base, green and red, decorated with stenciling, seating dressed figures of a girl and a boy with tin painted faces and jointed flat tin legs; clockwork inside base. Labeled on paper strip "PATENT APPLIED FOR."

15-1 Pair of Clowns on Red Wooden Seesaw
Maker undetermined
Possibly France, c. 1900
7½" x 3¼" x 6½"

Pair of dressed clowns, each with wooden limbs and white papiermâché head in peaked cap; connected to one another by horizontal steel rod, and set on seesaw; seesaw made of red wooden bench set on red wooden cradle-rockers, with steel clockwork-and-block mechanism beneath bench. See-saw rocks as block moves up and down when clockwork is wound.

15-2 Clowns on Rotating Seesaw
Muller and Kadeder
Nuremberg, Germany, c. 1903
4" x 8" x 7¼"

Yellow tin cylinder with slide, seating clown at either end, rotating on vertical axle attached to clockwork beneath green stand; movable lead wheel attached by horizontal rod to axle and by vertical rod to one clown; seesaw rotates and moves up and down, sliding ball between clowns when clockwork is wound.

15-3 Clowns on Rocking Cradle
Muller and Kadeder
Nuremberg, Germany, c. 1903
7" x 3" x 5½"

Two clowns (molded tin halves soldered together, with flat-cut movable arms and legs); lead weight and clockwork between rockers. Cradle rocks and clowns' arms move back and forth when clockwork is wound.

15-4 "Never-Stop See-Saw"
Gibbs Mfg. Co.
Canton, OH, c. 1905
L. 13", H. 13¾"

Red tin seesaw, seating boy in red and white and girl in blue (each made of molded tin halves soldered together) revolving on steel rod axle running along seesaw; seesaw balances on accordion-bent strip set vertically into blue stand with red and yellow stripes. Boy and girl twirl upright, then seesaw down strip of tin when toy is turned upside down. Impressed "PAT'D SEP. 16. 1903."

15-5 Parallel Slides with Cars
Maker undetermined
Possibly France, c. 1905
13" x 4" x 5"

Parallel varnished tin slides, soldered to parallel semi-revolving axle; clockwork at foot of one of supporting posts with grooves suspended from slides to act as runners for two off-center wheels on second parallel axle. Slides move up and down alternately, rolling tin cars back and forth when clockwork is wound.

15-6 Seesaw behind Proscenium
Maker undetermined
France, c. 1905
5¼" x 1¼" x 3¼"

Gilded tin proscenium, elaborately decorated with pillars, center-piece, and urns; two gilded tin figures on seesaw visible in front of backdrop through stages. Seesaw moves up and down as attached nail is moved from behind.

15-7 "Teeter Kids Toy"
Gibbs Mfg. Co.
Canton, OH, c. 1915
7½" x 2¾" x 6¾"

Doubly bent steel rod suspended through cradle swinging on tin ax-le at top of swing stand; seating boy in red jacket and yellow boots and girl in green dress (molded halves soldered together). La-beled "GIBBS TOY MADE IN U.S.A. PAT. PEND."

16 | Carousels

The theme of European fancifulness and love of display (as com-pared to American attitudes) is demonstrated even more forcefully with the German and French carousels which were popular in America during the years 1880-1910. Here decorativeness is as im-portant as depiction of a scene or of action. Various kinds of cloth, used in combination with flags, medallions, decals, pompoms and assorted gingerbread trim, almost overwhelm the horses, riders, and other figures in some. In others, such as the carousel with balloons and dirigibles and the clowns holding a carousel (16-9, 16-8), the ef-fect is almost surrealistic. Contrast the Althof, Bergmann carousel (16-1), which is tame in comparison—though admittedly it is earlier than the others—a German idea which has been played down for the American taste, perhaps?

In collecting these toys, the collector must be watchful for missing parts and replacements. Rarely will a complete toy in perfect condi-tion be found. The sad state in which these toys often appear is part-ly explained by the fact that they are composed of many separate—

and separable—parts and further by the simple wear and tear of operation. The cloth parts, quite naturally, will be those most likely to fade and deteriorate—or to be missing completely.

This is one of the areas where a conscious decision must be made whether to restore missing or shabby parts—and, if so, what criteria to use. If it is decided to restore such a toy, the old maxim "Do not do what you cannot undo" is helpful. Removed parts should be kept for the time when the toy might be resold and also might prove invaluable if the collector later determines that the toy should be restored in another way.

16-0 Carousel with Gingerbread Trim and Horse-Head Medallions
(color plate)
Maker undetermined
Germany, c. 1880-1910
Diam. 7½", H. 15½"

Tin carousel, with white gingerbread-trimmed stand, containing yellow revolving disk, four exterior posts decorated with gilt double-horse-head medallions, and central pole supporting white tin canopy; three lithographed tin horses with riders; set on vertical steel poles soldered to disk; disk turned by iron cogwheels connected to cast-iron pulley wheel at side. Carousel works with steam engine or motor.

16-1 Carousel with Parian-Ware Doll
Althof, Bergmann and Co.
New York, NY, c. 1870
Diam. 19½", H. 15½"

Blue tin carousel, on finished wooden platform; umbrella wheel rotating on vertical axle projecting from stand, with white linen canopy cover featuring wool trim and tin flag; cars and horses suspended on bent double rod from spokes of umbrella wheel; doll with parian-ware head "turning" crank connected to clockwork inside stand.

16-2 Gymnasts on Revolving Disk
Maker undetermined
Possibly France, c. 1870-90
D. 4¼", H. 7¼"

Painted tin disk revolving with center pole and gold globe beneath multi-colored canopy; four gymnasts, two men with sticks and two women with hoops, each connected through disk at one foot to rod revolving on horizontal wheel rotating around green stand; clockwork beneath stand. Disk rotates and gymnasts revolve when clockwork is wound.

16-3 Carousel with Velvet Canopy
Maker undetermined
Possibly France, c. 1880
Diam. 12", H. 16¼"

Painted tin carousel, with green stand, red central pillar, and umbrella wheel rotating on axle projecting from top of pillar; velvet roof decorated with silver tin decals, pom-poms, and flags; four seats with two tin passengers each and four pairs of horses with jockeys suspended on rods swinging from spokes of umbrella wheel; clockwork beneath stand.

16-4 Carousel with Swings and Plaster Riders
Maker undetermined
Possibly Germany, c. 1880
Diam. 4", H. 9½"

Carousel, composed of green disk tin with white revolving vertical pole and canopy between three yellow rigs; three seats with plaster passengers suspended on curved double rods from canopy; clockwork beneath disk.

16-5 Steeplechase "Caroussel"
Maker undetermined
Germany, c. 1880-1900
6¼" x 6¼" x 10"

Painted, gilded, and lithographed tin carousel, composed of yellow disk rotating on vertical rod with horizontal red central disk and red canopy; two lithographed jockeys and horses soldered to yellow disk and two gilded seats with lithographed passengers suspended from either end of rod soldered across red disk; set between large openwork bow on square green stand. Labeled "Caroussel . . ."

16-6 Amusement Ride
Maker undetermined
Possibly Germany, c. 1890
12" x 12" x 13"

Painted and lithographed tin pedestal with three projecting sections revolving on axles attached to vertical wheels rotating around disk on top of pedestal; two detachable seats with passengers sitting opposite one another, suspended from ends of rotating sections; clockwork beneath pedestal.

16-7 Carousel with Inverted Roof
Maker undetermined
Possibly Germany, c. 1890-1910
Diam. 6", H. 12"

Lithographed and painted tin carousel, off-white, with cylindrical base-stand, center pillar, and multi-colored peaked inverted roof decorated with gingerbread trim; three carousel horses and riders, lithographed tin; set on steel rods soldered to revolving disk within base-stand; music box and clockwork beneath pillar.

16-8 Clowns Holding Carousel
S. Gunthermann
Nuremberg, Germany, c. 1900
9" x 4½" x 12"

Tin clown lying on back, dressed in red and yellow costume, supporting carousel on pole with body. Carousel has four suspended tin canoes with propellers and passengers and spins when clockwork mechanism is wound. Second clown holds banjo, similarly activated.

16-9 Aerial Carousel
Maker undetermined
Germany, c. 1910
Diam. 11", H. 14½"

Green tin stand with white central
pillar and two overlapping tin
canopies; three lithographed tin
balloons, suspended from smaller
canopy, and three zeppelins and
three airplanes suspended by
doubly bent rods from larger
canopy; clockwork beneath
stand and music box within pillar.
Labeled "GES. GESCH."

17 | Ferris Wheels

French lightness and delicacy (if generalizations about national
characteristics have any validity) are the hallmark of the ferris wheel
illustrated in color. The toy is small, its intricate design is painstaking-
ly executed, and it is finished in a solid gilt color. Contrast this with
the painted cast-iron American ferris wheel shown in illustration 17-4.

The point here is not that European toys of the late nineteenth and
early twentieth centuries are better (or worse) than American toys;
the point is rather that the American toy-manufacturing tradition is
only one of several which developed during the period covered
and that other traditions contained markedly different attitudes
towards design, different construction and finishing techniques,
and different ideas as to what the proper purposes of a toy are.
These contrasting traditions will be seen existing side by side
throughout many of the remaining sections of this book, and cross-
currents of influence on each by the other will also be noted.

17-O "Grande Roue de Paris" Ferris Wheel on Stand with Wheels
  (color plate)
Maker undetermined
France, c. 1900
5" x 3½" x 6¾"

Gilded tin ferris wheel, comprised of twelve closed cars revolving with
openwork wheel on axle set between two rigs; rigs set on stand em-

bossed with crosshatching, and stand in turn set on four pewter wheels with steel axles; with pewter pulley wheel on one axle, attached by string pulley to wheel on ferris wheel's axle. Ferris wheel rotates as toy is drawn along. Impressed on stand "DEPOSE 1900 J.S." and "GRANDE ROUE DE PARIS."

17-1 Ferris Wheel with Clown-Pumped Motor
Maker undetermined
Possibly France, c. 1900
11½" x 5½" x 10"

Ferris wheel consisting of blue tin brace-frames each with one suspended multi-colored tin seat with gingerbread trim and three plaster riders; brown and olivegreen tin platform supporting orange tin motor box containing plink-plonk box; clown (molded tin halves clasped together), attached to clockwork mechanism. Clown pumps handle to motor box, pulleys turn ferris wheel, and plink-plonk box plays when clockwork is wound.

17-2 Ferris Wheel with Arched Bows
Maker undetermined
Germany, c. 1900
10" x 5½" x 14"

Off-white tin ferris wheel, revolving around axle attached to large arched bow over wheel; bow connected to two smaller bows on either side; six tin and steel rod seats with passengers; barrel on one side of large bow contains music box and clockwork.

17-3 Ferris Wheel with Three Seats
Maker undetermined
Possibly Germany, c. 1900
6" x 4¾" x 9¼"

Red and blue painted tin ferris wheel, with pale blue roof, revolving around axle between two posts, on green and yellow stand; three seats, with female passengers; clockwork attached to one post.

17-4 Ferris Wheel on Bank Base
Possibly Hubley Mfg. Co.
Lancaster, PA, c. 1895
5½" x 16½" x 21¼"

Ferris wheel, modeled after one at Columbian Exposition, on penny bank base with clockwork mechanism. Black cast-iron braces support tin wheel with six tin seats each holding two cast-iron passengers in derby hats. Coin activates toy. Labeled in relief on bottom "BOWENS PAT APD FOR."

17-5 "Ferris Wheel Bank" with Motor House
Possibly Hubley Mfg. Co.
Lancaster, PA, c. 1895
5" x 15½" x 17"

Clockwork-operated ferris wheel on black cast-iron bank base with simulated brick motor house. Two black cast-iron braces support red and black tin wheel with five yellow cast-iron swinging back-to-back benches, each with two cast-iron passengers. Coin placed in roof of house activates mechanism.

17-6 Ferris Wheel and Power House
Maker undetermined
France, c. 1900
7³/₄" x 4" x 6¹/₂"

Gilded tin ferris wheel, with twelve closed cars, revolving on axle between two gilded rigs; flat rim on one side to act as surface for lead wheel connected to clockwork inside power house (red and gray lithographed tin with simulated brick smokestack); flat wooden stand covered with yellow lithographed paper.

18 | Bell Toys

Louis Hertz has defined bell toys as those "which when drawn or pushed along the floor ring a bell at intervals, either by internal motion or by the action of animated figures on the toys." Some of them are made of tin, wood, and stamped steel, but most of them are made of cast iron. Their range of styles varies from the very simple (18-3) to the complex (18-12). They often exhibit explicit themes of one kind or another, drawing from history, fables and fairy tales, and even the Bible.

The earliest bell toys appeared in the 1870s and are composed of stamped tin animals and figures, much like those in sections 2 and 3, and possess the naïve charm of toys of that period. These are rather scarce and highly prized.

The quintessential bell toys, however, are the elaborate ones made in the 1880s and 1890s. These produce not only the expected clanging, but also a surprising variety of action: Punch hits Judy and she falls into a well (and a bell rings); a clown and a poodle frolic (and the poodle rings a bell); clowns seesaw back and forth (to the tune of a ringing bell); a dignified eagle hovers on a chariot (with a ringing bell in its beak); and Jonah emerges from the whale's mouth (yes, with tintinnabulation).

The action portions of these toys are quite similar to that of mechanical banks of the period. Several concerns such as the Gong Bell Manufacturing Company of East Hampton, Connecticut, specialized in the manufacture of these toys almost exclusively. For whatever reason, by 1900 the elaborate bell toys seem to have fallen out of favor. Twentieth-century bell toys tend to be less dimensional, are usually made of stamped steel or wood rather than cast iron, and often portray historical and comic characters.

Bell toys are a collectible category in their own right and also provide materials for collectors of toys in other prototype categories. They are also interesting simply as an indication of manufacturing inventiveness and an evocation of period humor.

18-O "Punch and Judy" (color plate)
Maker undetermined
U.S.A., c. 1880-1910
10¼" x 3¾" x 6½"

Brown cast-iron platform decorated with gilt trim and stars; set on four ornate cast-iron wheels, and labeled "PUNCH AND JUDY." Hollow well over front axle contains cast-iron figure of Judy, connected by iron rod to bend in axle; figure of Punch, with steel rod, similarly connected. When toy is pulled, Punch appears to strike Judy with rod, she sinks into well, and bell rings.

18-1 White Horses with Twin Bells
Maker undetermined
U.S.A., c. 1850-1900
8¾" x 4½" x 7¼"

Pair of white tin trotting horses, each set on brace by tab at stomach; brace inserted through rectangular green stand on four iron wheels and attached to bend in back axle by eccentric rod; mushroom-shaped gilt iron bells on stand. Brace with clappers rocks back and forth, making horses trot and hitting bells when toy is pulled.

18-2 Horse-Drawn Pink Blossom
Maker undetermined
U.S.A., c. 1880-95
10¾" x 3¾" x 6¾"

Large pink cast-iron open blossom set on two large iron wheels; mushroom-like steel bell rising from one side of blossom, stem connected to rod touching bend in wheel axle; three rotating iron spokes with suspended lead clappers screwed to top of bell by brass finial; attached by shafts and floral float to rearing horse with seated boy. Clappers strike bell when toy is pulled.

18-3 Horse-Drawn Bell on Wheels
Maker undetermined
U.S.A., c. 1880-1910
11½" x 3½" x 4½"

Steel bell, rotating on axle between two large nickel-plated cast-iron wheels, attached by tin shafts to cast-iron trotting horse; set on immobile balancing wheel. Bell rings when toy is pulled.

18-4 Bells with Flags on Three-
Wheeled Platform
Maker undetermined
U.S.A., c. 1880-1910
4¾" x 2½" x 4¼"

Tin platform, with small lead balancing wheel and two tin wheels on each side, supporting two steel bells with brass finials and red and yellow steel flags; double-headed lead hammer clapper activated by lead tab on wheel axle. Clapper strikes bells when toy is pulled.

18-5 Boy Catching Fish
Maker undetermined
U.S.A., c. 1890-1910
8" x 3¾" x 6"

Cast-iron barefoot black boy sitting on tree trunk holding steel fishing rod attached to silver-colored fish; cast-iron platform depicting pool and grass with slot for fish. Boy's arms lower and raise rod and fish when toy is pulled. Platform labeled "PAT APLD FOR" in relief.

18-6 "Evening News Baby Quieter"
J. and E. Stevens Co.
Cromwell, CT, c. 1893
7¾" x 3¾" x 5¾"

Copper-colored cast-iron chaise lounge, with molded detail; set on two large copper-plated iron wheels and one small balancing wheel with seated cast-iron man dressed in smoking jacket, high collar, and trousers, holding rattle, and reading "EVENING NEWS BABY QUIETER," with movable leg supporting baby in smock; man's leg attached by mechanism to bell clapper. Man lifts and lowers leg and baby, and clapper strikes bell, when toy is pulled.

18-7 "No. 50 Eagle"
Gong Bell Mfg. Co.
East Hampton, CT, c. 1895-1903
5¾" x 3½" x 4"

Open-work green cast-iron frame with "NO. 50 EAGLE" in gilt relief; set on four ornate lead wheels; red, white, and blue eagle holding metal bell from mouth and pivoting on rod attached to tin tab on bend in wheel axle. Eagle moves from side to side, shaking bell, when toy is pulled.

18-8 "Poodle Dog Bell Ringer No 45"
Gong Bell Mfg. Co.
East Hampton, CT, c. 1903
8" x 3½" x 6¼"

Maroon platform, with "POODLE DOG BELL RINGER NO 45" in gilt relief; set on four iron wheels supporting pivoting cast-iron clown with one foot attached by rod and tab to bend in back axle, and supporting white cast-iron poodle, pivoting on post and holding steel bell with copper clapper by rod in mouth. Clown and dog pivot back and forth and bell rings when toy is pulled.

18-9 "Daisy" Bell Toy
Gong Bell Mfg. Co.
East Hampton, CT, c. 1903
8" x 3½" x 6"

Green cast-iron sled, decorated with white horse figurehead and floral designs in relief, seating cast-iron girl dressed in coat and hat, with long hair, muff, and doll, draped with quilt; set on four silver-colored iron wheels; steel bell, with springs and loose internal clapper, between larger back wheels. Labeled in relief "DAISY."

18-10 "Ding Dong Bell"
Gong Bell Mfg. Co.
East Hampton, CT, c. 1903
9¼" x 3" x 5"

Brown cast-iron well, with "DING, DONG, BELL/PUSSY'S NOT IN THE WELL" in gilt relief; set on two simulated grassy ridges on four nickel-plated iron wheels, supporting at one end "nasty" boy with long nose and at other end "nice" boy holding white cat; nickel-plated bell suspended beneath roof of well and connected off-center by hooked rods to one wheel. Bell rings when toy is pulled.

18-11 "Pig with Clown Rider"
Gong Bell Mfg. Co.
East Hampton, CT, c. 1903
5¾" x 2½" x 4½"

White cast-iron pig; set on bend in steel axle of two ornate lead front wheels and tin back balancing wheel, carrying clown, holding pig's ears; bell suspended beneath. Pig rolls up and down and bell rings when toy is pulled.

18-12 White and Black Clowns
      Riding Seesaw
N.N. Hill Brass Co.
East Hampton, CT, c. 1905
6¼" x 3" x 4¾"

White cast-iron seesaw; set on copper-plate frame on four tin wheels, seating white clown in white, and black clown in yellow and red, partly rotating above steel bell, and connected to bend in wheel axle by rod. Clowns seesaw and ring bell when toy is pulled.

18-13 "Jonah"
N.N. Hill Brass Co.
East Hampton, CT, c. 1905
6" x 2¾" x 4"

Black cast-iron whale, with opening mouth containing Jonah in white gown attached to movable iron strips connected to front axle; bell beneath platform also connected to front axle and rung by iron strip on back axle; set on four iron wheels. Jonah slides in and out of whale's mouth and bell rings when toy is pulled. Labeled in relief "JONAH."

18-14 "Improved Fish Toy"
Gong Bell Mfg. Co.
East Hampton, CT, c. 1905
8" x 2¼" x 4¾"

Molded cast-iron fish with articulated scales and fin and with promi-
nent teeth in red mouth opening on axle with rod extending from rear
to touch bend in wheel axle; clown, rocking on rod attached to bend
in wheel axle holding metal bell on fishing rod; set on two cast-iron
wheels. Clown rocks back and forth shaking bell and fish opens and
shuts mouth when toy is pulled.

18-15 Horse and Clown on Bell Frame with Gear
N.N. Hill Brass Co.
East Hampton, CT, c. 1905
10" x 3¾" x 7"

Cast-iron clown in white and red polka-dotted suit and yellow hat attached to galloping cast-iron horse by rod connected at front wheel
axle; two steel bells suspended beneath; set on four tin wheels. Horse
and clown rock back and forth and bell rings when toy is pulled.

19 | Lithographed Wooden Toys

As a rough generalization, if a toy form was made in cast iron or tin in
the late nineteenth century, it was also made in lithographed wood.
The wooden toy, either covered with lithographed paper or with
printing inks directly applied, was the less expensive substitute.
Wooden fire engines, wagons, ships, trolleys—what-have-you—appeared in great array and were a colorful addition to the toy scene.

These toys seem to have been an outgrowth of the manufacture of
wooden building blocks, and most of them retain a rather blocky,
box-like character. The lithographed paper often includes added
"realistic" detail in its design, such as faces at the windows of
coaches and smoke emanating from cannons, which gives a car-
toon-like quality to these toys. The wood used is normally soft and of
rather poor quality and it is remarkable that these relatively perishable toys have survived.

The lithographed-wood toys made at the time of the Spanish-
American War (1898) are a most unique group; "models" of warships
were quickly designed and manufactured to capitalize on the news
event of the decade (19-6).

Among the makers of lithographed wood toys are Charles M. Crandall Co. of Montrose, Pennsylvania; W. S. Reed Toy Co. of Leominster, Massachusetts; Milton Bradley Co. of Springfield, Massachusetts; and Gibbs Manufacturing Co. of Canton, Ohio.

The popularity of these toys seems to have waned by the early 1900s, though some continued to be made thereafter. In general, they are more interesting in comparison to what they were copying than as a category in themselves.

19-0 "Central Park" Liliputian Railway Coach (color plate)
W.S. Reed Toy Co.
Leominster, MA, c. 1877
Streetcar, L. 14½"; horses, L. 10½"

Street car of polychrome-lithographed paper on wood labeled "CENTRAL PARK," "BROADWAY" and "REED'S LILIPUTIAN RAILWAY COACH," with silver-striped double-tiered roof, containing ten passengers of lithographed paper on cardboard; set on four red wheels; pulled by two horses with shafts and front wheels of lithographed and printed wood; detachable descriptive sign on second tier.

19-1 "Crandall's Happy Family"
Charles M. Crandall Co.
Montrose, PA, c. 1876
18" x 5½" x 7¾"

Zoo cage, wooden with steel bars, styled "CRANDALL'S HAPPY FAMILY," featuring back covered with paper print of jungle scene; containing fifteen animals and two trees printed on flat-cut wood and set upright into grooves cut into bottom of cage, some with leather tails and some with jointed limbs. Labeled "(CRANDALL'S IMPROVED BUILDING BLOCKS.) Patented February 5th 1867. Reissued March 30th, 1875, and May 4th, 1875. Patented October 11th, 1875. Patented January 25th, 1876."

19-2 "Pansy" Stagecoach with Four-Horse Team
Possibly W.S. Reed Toy Co.
Leominster, MA, c. 1877
L. 29"

Wooden stagecoach with polychrome-lithographed paper on yellow background, lithographed on each side, with raised back and front benches; set on four large back wheels with projecting hubs and lithographed spokes; pulled by four lithographed wooden horses attached to long red wooden shafts hinged at chassis-end and middle. Labeled "PANSY" above door.

19-3 Horse-Drawn Fire Engine with Lithographed Sides
Possibly W.S. Reed Toy Co.
Leominster, MA, c. 1877
Fire Engine, L. 14¾"; horse, L. 15"

Fire engine, polychrome-lithographed paper on wood and cardboard, attached by shafts on front wheels to similar horse, with detachable boiler and cover, front and back drivers, and detachable steam ejector and posts.

19-4 "Jackson Park" Chicago Trolley Car
Possibly W.S. Reed Toy Co.
Leominster, MA, c. 1893
17½" x 6½" x 9"

Polychrome lithographed on wood and cardboard trolley car, labeled "JACKSON PARK VIA GRAND BOULEVARD," with double-tiered roof, two movable antennae attached to bottom of car by strings; set on four wheels; names of trolley stops around perimeter of upper tier: "WORLD'S-COLUMBIA-EXPOSITION," "PRAIRIE AV.," "LINCOLN PARK," and "STATE ST.," with driver and brakeman of lithographed paper on wood.

19-5 "Hercules" Railway Locomotive and Car
Milton Bradley Co.
Springfield, MA, c. 1881
L. 45¾"

Steam-type locomotive, 4-4-0, polychrome lithographed, depicting engineer in cab with two windows on each side; labeled "HERCULES"; polychrome-lithographed passenger car, labeled "ATLANTIC AND PACIFIC" and "City of Springfield," depicting passengers behind windows with blinds; set on two pairs of four wheels; coal car, black and brown painted wood. Labeled "MILTON BRADLEY & CO. BUILDERS, SPRINGFIELD MASS" and "1881" on each side.

19-6 Battleship "Terror"
Maker undetermined
U.S.A., c. 1890-1900
22½" x 6½" x 10½"

Battleship of lithographed paper on wood with two decks, black wooden cannons, string rigging and U.S. flag at bow; set on four wheels; stylized depictions of Marines, ocean waves, and other details. Labeled "TERROR."

19-7 "Hook and Ladder" Wagon with Horses
Gibbs Mfg. Co.
Canton, OH, c. 1900-20
21" x 3¾" x 8½"

Red wooden wagon, printed in black "HOOK AND LADDER FIRE DEPT." on both sides, with floral vine motifs, open top supporting two flat ladder braces; set on four green tin wheels with steel axles, pulled by pair of flat-cut wood lithographed horses with legs jointed at shoulders and hips, front legs set by eccentric pin on pair of tin wheels. Horses' legs walk when wagon is pulled.

19-8 "Pony Pacer"
Gibbs Mfg. Co.
Canton, OH, c. 1915
7½" x 2¾" x 2½"

Red tin sulky with silver cast-iron wheels; connected by tin rods to pony of lithographed papered and flat-cut wood, with movable screw-jointed tin legs held off ground by curved rod. Pony's legs move when cart is pulled.

19-9 "Pony Circus Wagon"
Gibbs Mfg. Co.
Canton, OH, c. 1915
13" x 3¾" x 6½"

Painted and lithographed papered wood and tin circus wagon, labeled "PONY CIRCUS WAGON No. 53"; orange, yellow and blue, on yellow tin with silver cast-iron wheels, connected by tin rods to two ponies of lithographed papered and flat-cut wood, with movable screw-jointed tin legs. Ponies' legs move in unison when wagon is pulled.

20 | Automatons

"Automaton" literally means "self-moving." The term as used by toy collectors generally is restricted to figures of animals or humans which appear to "act of themselves" by means of concealed motive power. Realism in appearance and action, and ingenuity in design and theme, are the standards by which they are judged.

Automatons have been favorites in continental Europe for centuries. Paris and Vienna were centers of fashion from which their popularity spread. In nineteenth-century America, many automatons were still imported, but the United States was also beginning to turn out its own distinctive variety.

European automatons (20-1, 20-2) tended to be either showcase pieces of aristocratic loveliness (woman at piano) or else caustic, satirical pieces bordering on the macabre (monkey dancing master). Americans adapted the form to fit their own tastes, however, and by 1875 or so were manufacturing tasteful domestic scenes extolling middle-class family life (see color plate 20) and representative everyday scenes (20-5). Caustic humor was there too, but it seems to have been reserved for minorities, chiefly blacks, who were the brunt of countless jibes delivered by American toymakers.

The virtuosity of mechanical design in all of these figures deserves comment. The clockwork is wound and, as if by magic, hands, legs, and heads move smoothly and naturally and the toys go through their assigned tasks, not jerkily or hastily, but in a smooth, natural rhythm. The combination of wheels, cogs, springs, cams, rods, string, elastic bands and other apparatus which is assembled to produce this result is astoundingly complex in the more complicated pieces and makes one appreciate the ingenuity of the Victorian mind.

The American company most closely identified with automatons is Ives, Blakeslee & Co., and several examples of Ives figures are shown here.

20-0 Woman Fanning Baby in Cradle (color plate)
Maker undetermined
Possibly Automatic Toy Works
New York, NY, c. 1882
8" x 5" x 9½"

Doll figure of woman with papier-mâché head, dressed in cotton and lace clothes and holding paper fan, leaning over wooden cradle and holding diminutive doll figure with china head, also dressed in cotton and lace. Clockwork, connected to large doll, is contained in lacquered wooden box. Cradle with baby rocks and woman leans over to push cradle while turning head when clockwork is wound.

20-1 The Dancing Master
Maker undetermined
Possibly France, c. 1850
5¼" x 4¼" x 14¾"

Monkey doll, with papier-mâché head, hands, and legs, with opening mouth, dressed in elaborate costume including satin waistcoat, silk tails, wooden cane, and metal eyeglasses; with four tin keys working mechanism inside box connected to right arm, mouth, and head of monkey. "Dancing master" holds eyeglass up to eye, nods head, opens mouth, and turns head as each key is individually depressed.

20-2 Woman in Velvet Dress Playing Piano
Maker undetermined
Possibly Germany, c. 1870
8½" x 6½" x 9"

Doll figure of woman with papier-mâché head and arms, dressed in blue velvet gown with black lace overgown, seated at wooden upright piano with wooden keys and decorated with gilt stenciling; set on wooden box covered with decorative printed paper and containing music box mechanism worked by enamel crank outside box. Doll moves realistically and sways back and forth over keyboard, and music box plays elaborate melody, when clockwork is wound.

20-3 "Monkey Churning"
Ives, Blakeslee and Co.
Bridgeport, CT, c. 1870-93
7¼" x 4½" x 11"

Monkey figure with papier-mâché head, hair-covered limbs and cast-iron feet, and dressed in colorful cloth costume; hands attached together at vertical rod moving up and down in orange wooden churn; monkey and churn set on lacquered wooden box containing clockwork. Monkey bends up and down with churning rod when clockwork is wound.

20-4 Boy in Silk Cap and Jacket
Riding Velocipede
Ives, Blakeslee and Co.
Bridgeport, CT, c. 1870-93
8½" x 4½" x 9½"

Doll figure of boy—with cloth composition head, tin hands and boots, and wooden torso dressed in silk, lace, and velvet—seated on wooden, iron, and tin velocipede with white tin horse's head above pivoting iron front wheel and lacquered wooden steering levers connected off-center to iron back wheels; boy's feet connected to front wheel and hands connected to levers; brass and steel clockwork beneath seat. Velocipede's wheels turn and boy's hands move back and forth with levers when clockwork is wound.

20-5 Old Woman and Boy of Peddler's Wagon with Horse
Ives, Blakeslee and Co.
Bridgeport, CT, c. 1874
17" x 4¼" x 10"

Figure of old woman with papier-mâché head and tin arms, dressed in pink cotton dress, wood apron, kerchief and shawl, and black boy with papier-mâché face on wooden head, with cast-iron legs, dressed in tin hat and wool jacket and knickers; woman in seat of and boy at back of red and yellow tin peddler's wagon pulled by tin horse; clockwork beneath wagon. Woman jiggles and boy walks, pushing wagon, when clockwork is wound. Labeled "Patented March 7, 1871, and April... 1874."

20-6 Black Man Bouncing Beneath Canopy
Maker undetermined
U.S.A., c. 1875
5¼" x 4½" x 9½"

Puppet, representing black man, with papier-mâché head and dressed in bright clown costume; jointed wooden hands and legs in black boots; suspended by hook from brass, steel, and iron clockwork with flywheel beneath draped and lacquered wooden canopy suspended from wooden pillar on wooden stand. Puppet bounces up and down on platform when clockwork is wound.

20-7 Elephant Cranking Music Box with Drum
Maker undetermined
Possibly Germany, c. 1880
13" x 7½" x 10½"

Felt-covered elephant, with velvet tasseled coverings, ivory tusks, and glass eyes, attached by foot to treadle and by trunk to crank on wooden music box containing clockwork; box supports gilt and copper-colored tin drum with parchment skins and cymbals and drumstick moving on brass rod connected to foot treadle. When clockwork is wound, elephant pumps crank with trunk to run music box and presses treadle with foot to hit drum.

20-8 "The Mechanical 'Stump Speaker'"
Ives, Blakeslee and Co.
Bridgeport, CT, c. 1880-93
6¼" x 4" x 10¼"

Doll figure of black politician, with papier-mâché head, glass eyes, wooden cigar and cast-iron hands and feet, dressed in white straw hat and clothes of satin, cotton, and wool, and holding steel and cotton umbrella and flat leather carpetbag, standing behind black cast-iron table; doll and table attached to lacquered wooden base containing clockwork. Speaker leans up and down while banging umbrella on table when clockwork is wound.

20-9 "Iron Walking Monkey"
Ives, Blakeslee and Williams Co.
Bridgeport, CT, c. 1882-93
L. 6", H. 4½"

Monkey in crawling position, with jointed cast-iron head and limbs, fur tail and skull, dressed in red printed cotton smock and bloomers with lace trim and red felt fez. Monkey crawls when pulled by string.

21 | More Clockwork Toys

This category includes a number of clockwork toys other than the automatons treated in the previous section and other than the numerous clockwork toys spread through categories such as trains, cars, comic strip toys and so forth. Clockwork was perhaps the most versatile and pervasive source of power and animation for toys throughout the period 1840-1940, the time span which this book covers.

These toys tend to be less naturalistic than those in the automaton class both in use of materials and in movement. Many are made of metal or wood and the source of their movement is somewhat less sophisticated and more obvious. Note, for instance, the exposed clockwork in the color illustration. These were toys to amuse and to surprise, but not to bewilder and amaze.

This type of toy was made in great quantity in Germany by many companies, the most noteworthy being E. P. Lehmann of Brandenberg (see, for example, 40-3) and by companies such as Fernand Martin of Paris. These relatively cheap foreign clockwork toys were sold in huge numbers in the years between 1900 and World War I. There were domestic versions also, but usually patterned closely after the foreign ones.

21-O Park Bench Musicians (color plate)
S. Gunthermann
Nuremberg, Germany, c. 1900
9¼" x 2½" x 5"

Three black painted tin musicians, with movable arms, on park bench, two with violins and one with bass violin, dressed in jackets and top hats; exposed clockwork mechanism and plink-plonk box on one end. Musicians "play instruments" with moving arms when clockwork mechanism is wound so as to activate revolving rod with tabs beneath bench.

21-1 Three Girls Dancing on Pedestal
Maker undetermined
Possibly La Grove, Kemp and Webb
New York, NY, c. 1873
7¼" x 4¼" x 12¾"

Three doll figures of black girls with papier-mâché heads set on wooden torsos, wooden arms painted with white gloves and jointed at shoulders, and wooden legs painted with white hose and jointed at hips and ankles, each attached by horizontal twisted-metal hook to rotating vertical steel pole, and pole set into wooden pedestal on varnished wooden box containing clockwork.

21-2 Kitten in Tin Beer Stein
Ives, Blakeslee and Williams Co.
Bridgeport, CT, c. 1893
Diam. 5¼", H. 9½"

White fur-covered figure of kitten, with yellow glass eyes, red tin tongue, and pale-blue satin collar; set into black and gilt-striped tin beer stein with plain wooden base; plain wooden stein top set on screw atop kitten's head; clockwork inside stein. From 1893 Ives catalog: "When wound the cat's head will rise slowly, force the cover up, protrude its tongue and suddenly drop back into the box."

21-3 Woman Pushing Baby Carriage
Maker undetermined
Germany, c. 1900
8" x 1¾" x 8"

Painted tin figure (molded halves clasped together) of blonde woman pushing baby carriage with sitting baby; steel clockwork in woman's torso. Small wedge raises and lowers balancing wheel, pushing woman and carriage when clockwork is wound; rods, attached by hook joints from axle to woman and baby, move baby back and forth.

21-4 Barber and Bald Customer
Fernand Martin
Paris, France, c. 1903
H. 8"

Painted tin figures (molded halves clasped together) dressed in cloth costumes and set on stand. Barber shakes a bottle and rubs bald man's head when clockwork is wound. Label on stand "ARTICLE FRAN-ÇAIS. . . ."

21-5 Dancing Couple
Maker undetermined
Germany, c. 1905
H. 8"

Separate painted tin figures (man and woman in evening dress) consisting of molded halves clasped together and then soldered to one another at hands and feet. Vertically sliding rod and balancing wheel attached to clockwork inside woman's body. Couple dances, swooping and whirling, when clockwork is wound.

21-6 Boxer with Ball on Spring
Maker undetermined
Possibly Germany, c. 1910
4" x 3¼" x 7¾"

Black boxer with lead head and torso and composition arms jointed at shoulders. Shoulder joints are connected by steel rods to clockwork inside composition stand. Boxer punches ball set on vertical wire spring when clockwork is wound.

21-7 Toreador on Bull
Maker undetermined
Possibly S. Gunthermann
Nuremberg, Germany, c. 1910
7" x 2½" x 6¼"

Painted tin figures (molded halves soldered together) of toreador and bull. Clockwork inside box beneath bull's body. Bull's head bucks and rider moves back and forth when clockwork is wound.

21-8 "Busy Lizzie" with Carpet Sweeper
Maker undetermined
Possibly H. Fischer and Co.
Nuremberg, Germany, c. 1920
H. 6¾"

Lithographed tin figure of woman with green hair in bun, dressed in white and orange polka-dotted dress with blue bib-apron, and movable arms pushing tin carpet sweeper; steel clockwork inside torso. "Lizzie" pushes sweeper when wound. Labeled on bottom "BUSY LIZZIE made in Germany U.S. Pat applied for Brit. Pat. appl for D.R.P.A."

21-9 Sentry and Dog
Maker undetermined
Possibly Germany, c. 1920
3¾" x 1¾" x 9"

Tin British grenadier sentry, dressed in red and white uniform, with shifting eyes, standing in yellow and orange striped "sentry box," connected by pivoting steel rod to tin dog, set on steel balancing wheel; clockwork inside box. When clockwork is wound, dog circles box, then reverses action while sentry shifts eyes.

22 | Toy Engines

The collecting of miniature engines is a specialty in itself. As soon as technology allowed, toymakers began incorporating movement mechanisms in their products. Clockwork and wind-up toys and toys which have moving parts which are activated by rolling or pushing have already been discussed and, of course, continue to be made even today. In the late nineteenth century, however, toymakers and the public became fascinated with the types of power sources which propelled real-life machines—especially steam engines, hot-air engines, and electric motors. Miniature working versions of these and other types of engines were sold independently and were also incorporated into various toys. Many of the engines are beautifully designed and crafted and are showcase items in their own right.

The Buckman Manufacturing Company of New York and the Weeden Manufacturing Company of New Bedford, Massachusetts, each produced lines of steam engines and steam toys so carefully and solidly made that many of them are still in working condition today. Many German firms, including Gebrüder Bing, Ernst Plank, and J. Falk, also made large quantities of engines and toys, many of which were exported.

The typical steam engine consists of a firebox with an alcohol or kerosene lamp, a boiler, and a steam chest for power storage connected to a pulley system or other apparatus which, in turn, can be connected to toy accessories of various sorts (see section 23). Less popular with collectors are the simpler hot-air or caloric engines (22-7). Electromagnetic engines (22-9) were also manufactured in large quantities. These utilize several coiled-wire construction techniques and operate on various voltages.

NOTE: All of these toy engines are potentially dangerous and should be operated only by one who understands the mechanics of them and the hazards involved.

22-0 Upright Weeden Steam Engine on Gray Stand (color plate)
Weeden Mfg. Co.
New Bedford, MA, c. 1927-35
8" x 4" x 10"

Upright steam engine composed of gilded brass-painted boiler on red steel firebox, black and rose-red stamped-steel firebox and brass whistle attached by pipe to gilt zinc steam chest; set on black stamped-steel brace stand. Printed on paper label "WEEDEN TRADE MARK REG. U.S. PAT. OFF."

22-1 "Frisbie's" Upright Steam Engine
Stevens and Brown Mfg. Co.
Cromwell, CT, c. 1872
Diam. 5", H. 8¾"

Upright steam engine composed of green bulb-shaped boiler set on three legs and decorated with red and blue escutcheon with gilt scroll trim, brace-frames at top of boiler supporting partly rotating red eccentric beam, brace at one side of boiler supporting gilt cast-iron and brass steam chest, and brace at other side of boiler supporting red cast-iron flywheel with pulley wheels. Impressed on boiler "FRISBIE'S PAT. . . ."

**22-2 Horizontal Weeden Steam
     Engine on Red-Brown Base
Weeden Mfg. Co.
New Bedford, MA, c. 1890-1910
6¼" x 5¾" x 6"**

Horizontal steam engine, composed of brass-plated boiler with die-cast chimney spout decorated with bands and simulated nails, black zinc steam chest connected to boiler by long brass pipe, and lamp. Embossed on boiler "WEEDEN TRADE MARK REG. U.S. PAT. OFF."

**22-3 Horizontal Steam Engine with Nickeled Platforms
Maker undetermined
Germany, c. 1900
12" x 5¾" x 13½"**

Horizontal steam engine composed of brass-plated boiler set on metallic blue stamped-steel firebox at one end and on black cast-iron brace at other end attached by pipe to blue stamped-steel steam chest and brass piston chest, firebox and brace both attached to black and red-striped cast-iron stand. Stamped on bottom "BAVARIA."

**22-4 Horizontal Steam Engine with Red Flywheel and Stand
J. Falk
Nuremberg, Germany, c. 1910
6½" x 4¼" x 8½"**

Horizontal steam engine composed of brass-plated boiler set on stamped steel firebox with open ends on red cast-iron stand on four feet, attached to axle with red flywheel. Front embossed with insignia of castle keep labeled "J.F. MADE IN GERMANY."

**22-5 "Noris" Upright Steam Engine with Copper-Colored
     Smokestack
Ernst Plank
Nuremberg, Germany, c. 1910
4" x 4" x 10¾"**

Upright steam engine composed of brass-plated boiler on nickel-plated stamped-steel rim of blue steel firebox with narrow silver- and copper-colored steel smokestack; brass steam chest attached by pipe to top of boiler. Tin plaque embossed with insignia of wheel and wings labeled "GERMANY E.P." and tin plaque on boiler embossed "NORIS."

22-6 Horizontal Hot-Air Engine with Gilt Lamp
Gebrüder Bing
Nuremberg, Germany, c. 1910
8¾" x 3¼" x 4"

Horizontal hot-air engine composed of steel hot-air chest projecting out of maroon steel piston cylinder set on edge of maroon and black lithographed box-stand. Labeled on box-stand "GBN BAVARIA" and "2DRGM," and impressed on piston rod "D.R.G.M."

22-7 Manual Hot-Air Engine with Green Flywheel
Kenton Mfg. Co.
Kenton, OH, c. 1925
8" x 6" x 5"

Horizontal hot-air engine composed of red hot-air chest set on four feet, with gilt hydrant on top and horizontal piston cylinder with nickel-plated piston rod attached by eccentric wheel at ninety-degree angle to horizontal axle on red brace-stand. Labeled in gilt relief "KENTON."

22-8 Red Electro-Magnetic Motor with Copper Coils
Maker undetermined
Possibly U.S.A, c. 1900
6½" x 4½" x 4½"

Electric motor, composed of red stand on four gilt feet with two parallel vertical red braces attached to sides of top; two copper-wire-coiled cores attached opposite one another on insides of braces. Impressed on wheel "B2."

22-9 "Little Hustler" Electro-Magnetic Motor
Voltamp Electric Mfg. Co.
Baltimore, MD, c. 1920-30
3½" x 2¾" x 3¾"

Electric motor composed of black cast-iron frame set on wooden stand, containing insulated-wire-coiled core inside bottom and rotating insulated-wire-coiled armature inside top. Steel plaque embossed "LITTLE HUSTLER."

23 | Engine Accessories

The metal-working shop, illustrated in color, states the theme for most engine accessories: work. The pulley on the side was attached by a cord of string, leather, or rubber to one of the miniature engines discussed in the previous section. When the engine turned, a frenzy of activity took place in the shop, each workman going about his assigned task with marvelous efficiency and determination. As the Victorian child played, he learned facts about various trades and was hopefully impressed that work was very high on the scale of proper values.

Both Weeden and Buckman made various sorts of attachments to go with their engines—and so did the German firms. Not all of these, however, centered on the ethic of work. In fact, almost any type of toy could be activated by an independent engine and it is surprising how many toys have on them the little telltale pulley wheels which show that they are engine attachments—or that they can be if desired. See, for instance, the carousel illustrated in color in section 16; it can be operated manually or hooked up to an engine.

In fact, some of the engine attachments are wholly comic in their appeal. The monkey climbing up the birdhouse (23-7), for example, was made for sheer amusement.

23-0 Metal-Working Shop (color plate)
Maker undetermined
Germany, c. 1890
16½" x 5¾" x 8¾"

Tin machine shop, lithographed in simulated brick with orange roof in tile relief and linoleum floor; containing five workmen standing in a row (molded halves clasped together), dressed in uniforms; each workman at a different machine, including furnace, anvil, sharpener, lathe, and grindstone; machines attached by rope pulleys to parallel pulleys on crossbar acting as axle.

23-1 Sawyer's and Sharpener's Shop
Weeden Mfg. Co.
New Bedford, MA, c. 1890
11" x 4¾" x 7¼"

Shop composed of plain iron frame and red tin roof; containing rotating circular saw, two shafts on wheel, and wooden revolving grindstone, each on table with ornate iron legs; each machine attached by pulley rope to parallel pulleys on steel crossbar acting as axle. Embossed "TRADE MARK WEEDEN."

23-2 Gymnast on Swing
Maker undetermined
Germany, c. 1890-1910
4½" x 3¼" x 9¼"

Lithographed tin gymnast with flat-cut arms jointed at shoulders and attached to swing suspended on two rods from axle of tall swing stand; axle connected by vertical crankshaft to gilded iron pulley wheel; set on painted green stand.

23-3 Sculptor with Statue
Maker undetermined
Germany, c. 1900
4¾" x 3" x 5"

Mustached sculptor dressed in gray sailor's cap, trousers, and black jacket (molded halves clasped together), with one movable arm holding wooden mallet; arm attached to axle attached by vertical rod to pulley wheel; on platform.

23-4 Worker at Pump Well
Doll et Cie.
Nuremberg, Germany, c. 1910
4¼" x 3" x 4"

Lead worker dressed in blue work-suit, cap, and tan apron, with steel arms jointed at shoulders and attached to vertical steel rod which in turn is attached to bend in axle of lead pulley wheel; pump handle attached by rod to bucket inside well on stand. Paper label printed "DC MADE IN GERMANY."

23-5 Trip Hammer with Green
Flywheel
Maker undetermined
Possibly Germany, c. 1910
3¾" x 2¾" x 3"

Lead-headed hammer, rotating on axle stand opposite black anvil, both set on lithographed red box-stand; extension of hammer handle bent at ninety-degree angle to touch looped steel axle parallel to hammer-axle; axle with green flywheel with pulley wheel rotating outside box-stand. Trip hammer strikes anvil repeatedly when flywheel is turned. Labeled on both ends "62."

23-6 Baker and Oven with Conveyor Belt
Doll et Cie.
Nuremberg, Germany, c. 1912
5½" x 4¼" x 5"

Oven of simulated brick, with white conveyor tray sloping into oval tub, tray with elastic cord belt supporting four paper plates with composition baked goods; baker standing beside belt. Baker pushes lever in and out of oven, and belt rotates along conveyor tray with baked goods pressing up oven door, when pulley wheel is attached to steam engine or motor. Paper label on tub printed "DC MADE IN GERMANY."

23-7 Monkey Riding Up Birdhouse Pole
Doll et Cie.
Nuremberg, Germany, c. 1912
5" x 3¾" x 11¾"

Birdhouse set on simulated bark pole on simulated mustard-brown wooden box-stand on earthenware platform; monkey with plush head and stuffed felt torso seated on tin elevating chair attached to counterweight suspended inside pole; tin bird set on axle attached to vertical rod suspended from bottom of hut; red and yellow cast-iron pulley wheel attached to side of box-stand. Monkey rides up pole, bird emerges from hut as monkey's chair presses up rod, and monkey suddenly slides back down with counterweight. Labeled with sticker "DC MADE IN GERMANY" and embossed "D.R.G.M. 1006670."

24 | Streetcars, Horse-Drawn

In the time-honored fashion, horse-drawn trolley toys followed in the tracks of the real things. As street railways flourished in the nineteenth century, so did the toys, some made of tin and some of cast iron and still others of wood (see section 19).

The tin streetcars are characteristically of simple bent sheet-tin construction with colorful painting and fancy labeling and gilding. As in other tin toys discussed, there are often fancy stamped or cut open-work windows, but accessory trim tends to be minimal or stylized. The horses, though, tend to be of the molded-tin variety, either soldered or clasped together, usually with fluid hand painting. Iron and steel are also used on the toys, mainly in the wheels, axles, and shafts. The general look of the toys is rather two-dimensional and boxy, but with a certain degree of flair and lightness.

The cast-iron streetcars are a different matter. They are generally heavy, thick, and rather lifeless. Where cast iron as a medium is used to model a figure with many curves, protruding volumes, and receding voids, it works well; but when, as here, it is used to portray something with very little articulation of form, the effect is rather leaden.

24-0 "City Passenger Car" (color plate)
Maker undetermined
U.S.A., c. 1850-1900
10¾" x 5½" x 6¾"

Tin streetcar, painted red, gray, and green and stenciled in gold on both sides "CITY PASSENGER CAR," with six miter-shaped cut windows on each side, open front and back, platforms and stairs at front and back; set on four iron wheels. Separate pair of black trotting horses, each 8" long, (molded halves soldered together) connected by band of tin.

24-1 "Metropolitan Line" Street-car
Maker undetermined
U.S.A., c. 1850-1900
L. 14¼"

Blue and red painted tin streetcar, stenciled "METROPOLITAN LINE," with arch-cut windows and overhanging roof, open front and back; set on black iron wheels. Galloping tin horse (molded halves soldered together), soldered to steel shafts.

24-2 Streetcar
Maker undetermined
U.S.A., c. 1850-1900
12" x 2¼" x 4"

Blue and red tin streetcar with open front and end, six cut windows on each side, on four cast-iron wheels; connected by curved rod harness to two trotting horses (molded halves soldered together).

24-3 "Broadway Car Line" Streetcar
Maker undetermined
U.S.A., c. 1880-1920
11¾" x 4" x 5"

Cast-iron streetcar, labeled "BROADWAY CAR LINE 712," with orange body and maroon and yellow roof, six square-cut windows and eight perforated vents on each side, platforms with stairs at each end and partially-rotating crossbar at front. Two animated galloping cast-iron horses set off-center on balancing wheels.

24-4 Streetcar
Possibly James Fallows and Sons
Philadelphia, PA, c. 1885
12" x 2½" x 4"

Painted and stenciled tin streetcar, yellow and red, with open front and back, six cut windows on each side; set on four cast-iron wheels; connected by rotating curved shafts to two trotting horses (molded halves clasped together). Labeled "PATD. FEBY. 27. 1883."

24-5 Small Streetcar
James Fallows and Sons
Philadelphia, PA, c. 1888
7" x 1½" x 2¾"

Gilded tin streetcar, with red ridged roof and four cut windows on each side; set on cast-iron wheels; connected by double-pronged harness to tin trotting horse (molded halves soldered together). Base impressed "IXL."

24-6 Penny Toy Streetcar
Maker undetermined
U.S.A. or Germany, c. 1890
10¼" x 2¾" x 3¾"

Gilt varnished tin streetcar friction toy, embossed with Chinese characters, with five cut windows on each side revealing five flat-cut blue-and-green-clothed passengers, platforms at each end supporting flat-cut bugler and man in green (rear platform on two gilt wheels supporting elevated gilt lead flywheel); two small walking tin horses.

24-7 "Consolidated" Streetcar
Wilkins Toy Co.
Keene, NH, c. 1890
8½" x 2¾" x 4¼"

Red cast-iron streetcar, labeled "CONSOLIDATED," with five square-cut windows and six perforated vents on each side, platforms with stairs on each end; set on four wheels. Animated galloping cast-iron horse with curved steel rod shafts, set off-center on balancing wheel, 5" long. Horse gallops up and down when toy is pulled.

24-8 Streetcar
Maker undetermined
Possibly Kenton Hardware Mfg.
**   Co.**
Kenton, OH, c. 1910
6½" x 1" x 2½"

Red cast-iron streetcar pull toy, with six arch-cut windows and six cut vents on each side, cut window and platform at each end; set on four wheels. Connected by shafts molded to black galloping horse with gilt molded harness.

25 | Trolleys and Buses, Automotive

The color illustration is a D. P. Clark & Co. friction streetcar modeled after an electric trolley, not a horse-drawn one. It works on the mechanical principle described in section 28. It is an exceedingly simple, almost crude, toy, but is a good example of the many friction toys which were popular at around the turn of the century. The leaf-like designs are especially interesting since such forms are rarely found on American tin toys.

A clockwork tin version of the automotive streetcar is shown in illustration 25-1, but it is the Ives tin trolley in illustration 25-6 which is perhaps more interesting, for it is a direct offshoot of the electric train industry and indeed was made for an 0-gauge track, has electric-train-type couplers, flanged wheels and an electric motor. The Knapp "Electric Traction" trolley in illustration 25-7 is similar in construction technique and intended use.

Lehmann's autobus (25-7) is included as a sort of comic relief. The German toy company seemed to be able to make light of every toy it copied (in spirit as well as weight) as this diminutive version shows. The lithographed detailing is remarkably good for a cheap toy, and it boasts real rubber tires and a barrel and spring mechanism.

And finally there is the cast-iron bus (25-8), the not-too-different forerunner of the ones we know today. Its tires have not deflated, but have sagged under the bus's weight over the years (they are solid rubber of a cheap variety), and many tires on toys such as this are found in this condition. As noted in section 24, the use of cast iron can be rather heavy in a squarish enclosed form and it is here.

25-O Streetcar with Flat Figures (color plate)
D.P. Clark and Co.
Dayton, OH, c. 1900-09
14¾" x 4½" x 6¼"

Orange and black tin streetcar friction toy, decorated with gilt striping and russet and gilt leaf-like designs, with tiered roof, wooden floor, seven square-cut windows and two doors with steps on each side, and open door at front and back. Four flat-relief half-figures in windows on each side. Set on four gilt iron wheels with black iron flywheel in middle, disguised by another set of non-operating tin wheels. Impressed "PAT'D NOV 2-1897."

25-1 "City Hall Park 175" Open-Air Trolley Car
Morton E. Converse and Co.
Winchendon, MA, c. 1897
16" x 5" x 9"

Painted tin open-air trolley clock-work toy, with yellow and tangerine-colored roof and sides, decorated with black stenciling, green interior and six lemon-yellow reversible benches decorated with red stenciling; pivoting black trolley wire at top, pivoting steel control-rods at each end; set on four black tin wheels, one pair pivoting; brass and steel clockwork beneath car. Labeled "CITY HALL PARK 175" on each end, with rotating signs labeled "CITY HALL PARK" and "UNION DEPOT."

25-2 Streetcar with Flat-Cut Passengers
D.P. Clark and Co.
Dayton, OH, c. 1900-09
13" x 4" x 6"

Tin friction street car, painted black, orange, and yellow, with open front and back, seven square-cut windows on each side with four flat-cut heads of female figures on each side; set on four cast-iron wheels with large black iron flywheel between them. [Another version of toy illustrated in color.]

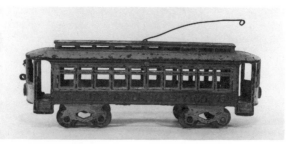

25-3 "National Transit Co." Trolley Car with Driver
Maker undetermined
Possibly Dent Hardware Co.

Fullerton, PA, c. 1905
11¾" x 2½" x 5½"

Yellow cast-iron trolley, with steel trolley wire, square-cut windows, perforated ceiling vents and doors with stairs on each side, enclosed platform with cut windows and simulated headlamps at each end; set on two pairs of four yellow wheels. Flat iron driver in blue uniform. Labeled in relief along brown panel "15 NATIONAL TRANSIT CO. 15."

25-4 Blue "Trolley" Car with Figures
Maker undetermined
Possibly Harris Toy Co.
Toledo, OH, c. 1905
7" x 2" x 6½"

Blue steel and cast-iron trolley car, labeled in gilt relief "TROLLEY," with gilt and maroon trim, six cut windows and six perforated vents on each side, platform with stairs at one end with molded conductor in blue uniform, and semi-enclosed platform at other end with molded driver similarly dressed; silver steel trolley wire at top.

25-5 "Lehmann's Autobus"
E.P. Lehmann
Brandenburg, Germany,
**   c. 1907-30**
8" x 3" x 5¼"

Lithographed tin double-deck bus, red and yellow, with curved staircase, seated driver dressed in brown at gilt steering wheel; set on four simulated rubber tires on pivoting joint; steel barrel and spring mechanism between back tires. Bus runs in circles when mechanism is wound. Labeled "LEHMANN'S AUTOBUS 590 MADE IN GERMANY LEHMANN'S MARKE D.R.G.M. PATD. U.S.A. 12. MAI. 03 & 22. Jany. 07 PATD. U.S.A. 13 SEPT. 1904 LEHMANN D.R. PATENT."

25-6 "Suburban" Track Trolley Car
Ives Mfg. Corp.
Bridgeport, CT, c. 1910-20
7½" x 2¼" x 5¼"

0-gauge tin trolley electric toy, labeled "SUBURBAN," with multicolored lithographed body and chassis; black iron cowcatchers on each end, steel hook-and-eye couplers; set on four tin-plate flanged wheels; electric motor inside body, attached to steel and wire trolley wire on top. Labeled "IVES No. 810."

25-7 "Electric Traction" Trolley Car
Knapp Electric Novelty Co.
New York, NY, c. 1910
10½" x 3¼" x 5"

Electric trolley, with yellow tiered tin roof and tangerine-colored tin sides, labeled in silver "ELECTRIC TRACTION," with steel hook coupler, six arch-cut windows on each side, platform with stairs with overhanging roof at each end, and wooden floor; set on black cast-iron chassis with four flanged copper-plated iron wheels on springs; electric motor between wheels; working glass and brass headlight connected to motor.

25-8 Green "Yellow Coach" Double-Deck Bus
Arcade Mfg. Co.
Freeport, IL, c. 1928
13" x 3¼" x 5"

Bus, printed "YELLOW COACH," with green cast-iron body, tin

floors, upper deck with tin seats,
lower deck with eight cut windows
on each side, curving staircase
between decks, and unpainted
cast-iron driver inside; set on four
rubber double tires.

25-9 "No. 721" Double-Deck Bus
Kenton Hardware Mfg. Co.
Kenton, OH, c. 1930
10" x 3¼" x 3¾"

Red cast-iron bus with black fenders; upper deck with twelve seats and
a bench; lower deck with eight cut windows on each side; turning
enclosed staircase between decks; with driver; decorated with various advertisements and signs.

26 | Trains, Pull Toys, Tin

The production of the first American tin pull-toy trains began in the
1830s and 1840s, shortly after the appearance on the scene of the
first real railroads. In general, their design and construction are dictated by two factors: the prototypes on which they were modeled
(which tended to be rudimentary) and the nature of sheet-tin construction (which does not allow for a great deal of modeling or three-dimensionality in the form), relieved somewhat by the addition of
certain cast-iron features such as wheels, cowcatcher, and other
components.

While the toy may be loosely based on an actual train, some features such as smokestacks, bells, and cabs are exaggerated, and
others, such as the "steam" mechanism itself, are minimized, giving
the toys an overall fanciful feeling. The decoration, often stenciled,
is elaborate, employing odd window shapes, floral and geometric
designs, and gilt. Finally, the trains are typically labeled with exotic
names in large letters.

Manufacturers included the Merriam Manufacturing Co. and the
firm of Hull and Stafford, both of Connecticut; Francis, Field & Francis
and James Fallow & Co. of Philadelphia; and Althof, Bergmann & Co.
of New York.

As with other tin toys, few are labeled; catalogs and company
records have been great aids in identification. (The exception,
again, is the Fallows "IXL" label.)

26-0 "Flash" Locomotive and Passenger Train (color plate)
James Fallows & Co.
Philadelphia, PA, c. 1883
L. 36"

Painted tin locomotive, with black boiler stenciled in gilt "FLASH" and impressed on front "A1," orange and black cab with blue roof and gilt indentations and stenciling, oval-cut windows on each side, black smokestack with gilt bell, and gilt cylinders with steel rod pistons; set on four iron wheels. Orange coal car, stenciled in gilt "R.R."; two orange passenger cars, stenciled in gilt "EMPIRE LINE."

26-1 Locomotive
Maker undetermined
U.S.A., c. 1850-1900
5¾"

Painted tin locomotive, with black boiler, yellow and orange cab with oval-cut windows on sides, and black smokestack; set on four small iron wheels.

26-2 "N.Y. & E.R.R." Railway Train
Maker undetermined
U.S.A., c. 1850-1900
L. 13"

Green painted tin coal car, with hook and eye couplers; set on four iron wheels. Yellow painted tin passenger car, stenciled in black "N.Y. & E.R.R.," with blue overhanging roof, closed front and back, steel railed platforms and steps, and four iron wheels.

26-3 "Fire Fly" Locomotive
Possibly Stevens and Brown Mfg. Co.
Cromwell, CT, c. 1870-72
L. 6½"

Painted tin locomotive, with brown boiler stenciled in gilt "FIRE FLY," blue cab with circular-cut windows on front and stenciled

windows on sides, black smokestack, and gilt cylinders with movable piston rods; set on four black
iron wheels.

26-4 "Lyon" Locomotive
Maker undetermined
Possibly Stevens and Brown Mfg. Co.
Cromwell, CT, c. 1870-72
L. 25¼"

Painted tin locomotive, with green boiler stenciled in gilt "LYON," black
smokestack and gilt bell, gilt cylinders with piston rods, cab with
circular-cut windows on front and gilt-stenciled windows on sides; set
on four black iron wheels. (Shown with mail and passenger cars.)

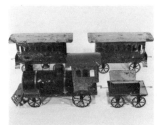

26-5 "Warrior" Railway
Locomotive
Maker undetermined
Possibly Ives, Blakeslee and
Co.
Bridgeport, CT, c. 1880
L. 48"

Painted tin locomotive with black
boiler stenciled in gilt "WARRIOR,"
orange cab with gilt stenciled trim
and three cut windows on each
side, black smokestack, gilt cylinders with steel pistons; set on four
ornate iron wheels; bell attached
beneath cowcatcher. Coal car,
stenciled in gilt "U.P.R.R.," with
hook couplers, and two passenger cars, each stenciled in gilt
"PALACE CAR," with eight cut windows on each side.

26-6 "Skip" Locomotive and Passenger Train
Maker undetermined
U.S.A., c. 1880-90
L. 13¼"

Painted tin locomotive, with black boiler stenciled in gilt "SKIP," gilt cab with rectangular-cut window on each side and black smokestack; set on four small iron wheels. Two passenger cars, each with stenciled panels, three ornate-cut windows on each side and cut entrances at front and back.

26-7 Small Locomotive and Passenger Train
Maker undetermined
U.S.A., c. 1880-90
L. 14¼"

Painted tin locomotive, with black boiler, orange cab without windows, and black smokestack; set on four small iron wheels. Two passenger cars, one blue and one orange, each with five arch-cut windows on each side, open front and back; and set on four iron wheels.

26-8 "Orion" Locomotive and Train
Ives, Blakeslee and Co.
Bridgeport, CT, c. 1883-93
L. 22½"

Painted tin locomotive, with black boiler stenciled in gilt "ORION," orange cab with oval-cut window on each side and blue roof with gilt stenciled trim, black smokestack and gilt cylinders with steel rod pistons; set on two ornate and two plain iron wheels, with steel bell suspended beneath front axle. Coal car, stenciled in gilt "R.R.," and passenger car with six arch-cut windows on each side. Impressed on passenger car "PAT.D FEB.Y 27. 1883."

26-9 Small Locomotive and Passenger Car Embossed with Stars
Maker undetermined
Possibly Germany, c. 1890
L. 8½"

Painted tin locomotive and coal car combined, with cylinder-and-funnel smokestack, embossed with stars; set on four wheels. Passenger car, with red roof and cut windows on each side, also embossed with stars.

27 | Trains, Pull Toys, Cast Iron

Cast-iron pull-toy trains began to appear in the 1880s or slightly earlier, and, as with other cast-iron toys, their manufacture was almost exclusively American. Their tin forerunners were fragile and, although possessing an undeniable charm, lacked the realism and sense of dynamism which the toy-buying public desired.

The manufacturing techniques for these toys were much the same as those for the other cast-iron toys discussed in earlier sections: sand-molded parts, bolted or pinned together, with raised modeling, usually painted overall and then the details accentuated with other colors or with gilt. The trains were set on cast-iron wheels, some of them with pivoting attachments. The best of these toys succeeded in their attempt to capture the "feel" of a real train—and as a group, they succeeded in capturing the pull-toy train market in the 1880s and 1890s.

Makers of the early models included the familiar names of Carpenter and Ives, and, in addition, the Wilkins Toy Co. of Keene, New Hampshire. Kenton, Hubley, Dent, Stevens, Harris, and several other companies also made these trains. It is interesting to note that Pratt & Letchworth, makers of the "Buffalo" brand, also made parts for real railroad trains.

Although we know, in general, the names of the companies which made these cast-iron trains, it is often difficult to assign a maker to a particular example, especially those made after 1900. The cheaper lines of several manufacturers became very similar in design and construction and in some cases almost identical. Copying seems to have become almost customary in the business, especially after certain patents on the earlier models ran out. These iron pull trains continued to be made in great numbers until the 1930s and even some of the latest ones look very "old." Detailing and care in construction tended to deteriorate, however, and a practiced eye can tell the difference.

27-0 Locomotive and "C.P.R.R." Gondola Train with Porters
(color plate)
Francis W. Carpenter
Port Chester, NY, c. 1890
L. 29"

Black steam-type locomotive, 2-4-0, with gilt ribbing, cowcatcher, headlamp, bell and steam ejector, and black smokestack and cylinders; set on black wheels with gilt hubs; black tender, with brad-like coupler; three orange and black gondola cars, labeled in relief "C.P.R.R."; three porters, each 3" high, in pastel-blue uniforms, set on disks with hooks to fit into holes in gondolas.

27-1 "999" Railway Locomotive and "Fast Express" Passenger Train
Maker undetermined
U.S.A., c. 1880-1920
L. 46½"

Steam-type black and gilt locomotive, 4-4-0, with steam ejector and whistle, ornate cut window on each side of cab, oval-cut window at front of cab, and double gilt steel piston rods connected to drive wheels and moving in and out of cylinders; black tender, labeled in gilt relief "999" with brad-like steel coupler; two orange passenger cars with black trim, labeled in gilt relief "FAST EXPRESS"; orange animal cage freight car with sliding doors.

27-2 Locomotive with Passenger Train and "Lulu" Tender
Maker undetermined
U.S.A., c. 1880-1920
L. 12¼"

Black steam-type locomotive, 2-2-0, with gilt trim and ribbing and rectangular-cut window at front of cab; connected to black tender on four wheels and labeled in gilt relief "LULU"; two orange parlor cars, with gilt embossed trim and brad-like steel couplers.

27-3 No. "178" Nickel-Plated Locomotive and "Lake Shore and Michigan Southern" Passenger Train
Maker undetermined
U.S.A., c. 1880-1920
L. 55¾"

Nickel-plated steam-type locomotive, 4-4-0, labeled in relief "178," with two arch-cut windows on each side of cab; nickel-plated tender, with two brad-like steel couplers, decorated with simulated nails; four nickel-plated parlor cars, labeled in relief "LAKE SHORE AND MICHIGAN SOUTHERN."

27-4 Black and Rose-Colored Railway Locomotive and Gondola Train
Francis W. Carpenter
Port Chester, NY, c. 1882
L. 19"

Steam-type locomotive, 2-2-0, with black engine and smokestack, two square-cut windows on each side of rose-colored cab, rose-colored cowcatcher, gilt steam ejector and brad-like coupler; orange tender and two rose-colored gondola cars. Labeled in relief "PATENTED. MAY 25. 1880. REISSUED MARCH 14. 1882."

27-5 Locomotive and Tender
Wilkins Toy Co.
Keene, NH, c. 1890
L. 21½"

Steam-type locomotive, 4-4-0, black with red and gilt trim, striped whistle and steam ejector, and double black movable steel piston strips connected to drive wheels; black tender, with iron T-shaped coupler, decorated with gilt striping and simulated nails along sides; set on two pairs of four red wheels; embossed star on each chassis. Labeled in relief "PAT. JUNE 19'[88?]."

27-6 Cast-Iron and Steel Locomotive and "New York Central & Hudson River" Passenger Train
Pratt & Letchworth
Buffalo, NY, c. 1892
L. 40"

Black steam-type locomotive, 4-4-0, with gilt, orange, and maroon trim, whistle and steam ejector; double steel piston rods, attached at drive wheels which move in and out of cylinders; black cast-iron tender, labeled in relief "P.R.R.;" orange steel baggage car with decorative label-

ing, platform with railings and
stairs at each end, and eye
couplers; orange steel passenger
car, with decorative labeling.

27-7 Locomotive with "189" Tender and "Union Line" Freight Car
Ives, Blakeslee and Williams Co.
Bridgeport, CT, c. 1893
L. 34¼"

Black steam-type locomotive, 4-4-0, with gilt molded ribbing, bell,
whistle, steam ejector, and jointed piston rods, attached to drive
wheels, which move in and out of two black cylinders; black tender,
labeled in relief "189," with gilt and red embossed trim; orange freight
car, labeled in gilt relief "UNION LINE" and "CAPACITY 50,000 LBS.,"
embossed with two gilt stars on each side, with simulated wooden
siding.

27-8 Locomotive and "MCRR" Gondola Train
Harris Toy Co.
Toledo, OH, c. 1903
L. 40½"

Black steam-type locomotive, 4-4-0, with molded ribbing, gilt cowcatcher, bell, whistle, steam ejector, and two arch-cut windows and
cut slot on each side of cab; black tender, labeled in gilt relief "976,"
with two brad-like steel couplers; two yellow gondola cars, labeled in
gilt relief "MCRR"; yellow caboose, labeled in gilt relief "CABOOSE
M.C.R.R."

27-9 Locomotive and "New York Central & Hudson River" Passenger
Train

Dent Hardware Co.
Fullerton, PA, c. 1905
L. 41½"

Black steam-type locomotive, 4-4-0, with gilt trim and molded ribbing, whistle, steam ejector, jointed pistons moving in and out of cylinders, and rectangular-cut window on each side of cab; black tender, with orange and gilt molded trim and brad-like coupler; two orange passenger cars, each with black trim, labeled in gilt relief "NEW YORK CENTRAL & HUDSON RIVER," with eight arch-cut windows and ten perforated vents on each side.

27-10 Nickel-Plated Locomotive and "Santa Fe Railroad Granague" Passenger Train
Kenton Hardware Co.
Kenton, OH, c. 1923
L. 37"

Nickel-plated steam-type locomotive, 2-4-0, with truncated smokestack, whistle, steam ejector, rectangular-cut window on each side of cab, and steel piston strips connected to rear wheels and moving in and out of cylinders; nickel-plated tender, with hooked bar coupler, decorated with simulated nails; two nickel-plated parlor cars, labeled in relief "SANTA FE RAILROAD" and "GRANAGUE"; similar observation car.

28 | Trains, Mechanized, Trackless

Trackless toy trains can be divided into several sub-categories, the most important of them being clockwork, live-steam, and friction models.

The clockwork models were produced as early as 1856 by George W. Brown & Co. in Connecticut. Sometimes a tin pull toy was fitted out with a clockwork mechanism—or, stated another way, sometimes the mechanism was omitted from a clockwork model and the toy was sold as a simpler and cheaper pull toy; both varieties can be perfectly legitimate.

Not surprisingly perhaps, Brown and some of the other early makers were also in the clock business and used some of the same mechanisms in their clocks and their toys. Later manufacturers, including Ives, Fallows and Althof Bergmann, obtained their mechanisms from independent clock companies. Clockwork mechanisms, with their combination of springs, wheels, gears and other mechanical movements, are varied and complex. They were designed to combine power with length of running time—and succeeded admirably; some of them will run up to an hour on one winding. Due to their complexity, however, these devices are difficult and expensive to fix when broken—and break they often did. Simpler wind-up mechanisms gained in popularity in the later years.

American live-steam trains were almost exclusively made to run on tracks (see next section), but it should be noted here that European trackless varieties (made in England, France, and Germany) did exist and were imported into this country from the 1870s to the early 1900s.

Friction trains (along with friction automobiles, trolleys, and other toys) were produced in large numbers from the 1890s to the 1920s and achieved the peak of their popularity during the middle decades of that period. In general, the friction toys are somewhat oversimplified in design, relying on their friction mechanism to hold interest.

The friction mechanism consists of a heavy flywheel connected to the drive wheel axle. When the toy is given several pushes along a flat surface, momentum builds up in the flywheel mechanism, and, when the toy is released, it will then run along the surface for some distance. Some of the early friction trains are made of wood, and the later ones tend to be made of wood and steel or entirely of steel.

28-0 "Red Bird" Locomotive (color plate)
Possibly George W. Brown & Co.
Forestville, CT, c. 1856-70
L. 8½"

Locomotive with black wooden base, orange tin boiler stenciled "RED BIRD," pink-white tin cab with yellow and black stenciled windows, black wooden smokestack and cowcatcher, and gilt cylinders with steel rod pistons; set on four iron wheels; brass and steel clockwork inside.

28-1 "The Rotary Railway Express"
Maker undetermined
England, c. 1850-90
L. 11¼"

Steam-type locomotive, 2-2-2, with green lead body and gilt lead smokestack, whistle, steam ejector, and grid; tender with green and gilt lead body and wire couplers; two parlor cars, one with red and silver lead body and one with brown and silver lead body. Accompanying clockwork mechanism causes toy to operate in circles on table top or other flat surface.

28-2 "Eclipse" Locomotive
George W. Brown & Co.
Forestville, CT, c. 1856
L. 9½"

Painted in locomotive with green boiler stenciled in gilt "ECLIPSE," yellow cab, orange ribbed roof and black stenciled windows, gilt bell, and yellow and black striped cowcatcher; set on balancing wheel at back and two red iron wheels at front.

28-3 "Union" Locomotive
George W. Brown & Co.
Forestville, CT, c. 1856-69
L. 8½"

Locomotive with wooden base, red tin boiler stenciled in gilt "UNION," yellow tin cab with stenciled windows, cylinders with movable steel rod pistons, and yellow wooden engine front supporting black wooden smokestack; set on balancing wheel and two green iron wheels; brass and steel clockwork inside engine.

28-4 Blue Locomotive with Embossed Decoration
Hull and Stafford
Clinton, CT, c. 1865
L. 8½"

Locomotive with turquoise-blue wooden base, red tin boiler embossed with scroll-work, turquoise-blue tin cab without windows, cushion-like roof, smokestack, gilt bell, and turquoise-blue cylinders with steel pistons; set on four orange iron wheels; brass and steel clockwork beneath.

28-5 "Excelsior" Locomotive
George W. Brown & Co.
Forestville, CT, c. 1870
L. 12"

Painted tin locomotive composed of yellow cab stenciled in black "EXCELSIOR," with ornate cut windows, black stenciled trim, and red roof and boiler with gilt whistle, steam ejector, bell and headlight, and tall black tapered-cylinder smokestack with knob on top; brass and steel clockwork and iron bell beneath boiler.

28-6 Locomotive with Bell Frame
Maker undetermined
Possibly Hull and Stafford
Clinton, CT, c. 1870-80
L. 7"

Painted tin locomotive with black boiler, red and blue cab with circular-cut windows on front and ornate cut windows on sides, red and gilt smokestack, and red cylinders with movable steel piston rods; set on four iron wheels, front wheels pivoting; brass and steel clockwork beneath locomotive.

28-7 Locomotive and "Union Pacific" Train
Ives, Blakeslee and Co.
Bridgeport, CT, c. 1870-83
L. 32"

Painted and lacquered tin locomotive with black boiler, orange cab with two ornate cut windows on sides and front, orange smokestack, cowcatcher, double-tiered whistle, gilt bell, and steel rod pistons attached to gilt cylinders; set on four ornate red cast-iron wheels; brass and steel clockwork beneath locomotive. Green with white-striped coal car, with decal of lion on each side. Orange passenger car on green base, stenciled in gilt "UNION PACIFIC R.R."

28-8 "America" Locomotive and Train
Maker undetermined
Possibly U.S.A., c. 1880
L. 22"

Painted tin locomotive with black boiler stenciled in gilt "AMERICA,"
with orange cab with ornate cut window on each side, black smokestack with orange cover, and blue cylinders; set on four iron wheels,
smaller front wheels pivoting; brass and steel clockwork in floor of cab.
Two passenger cars, one orange with blue ridged roof and one blue
with orange ridged roof.

28-9 "Boss" Locomotive and Train
Maker undetermined
U.S.A., c. 1880-90
L. 26"

Locomotive with black boiler stenciled in gilt "BOSS," gilt and orange
cab with heart-cut windows on each side, orange and gilt smokestack, and orange cowcatcher; set on four iron wheels; brass and steel
clockwork between back wheels. Green coal car, two orange and
gray passenger cars each stenciled "UNION PACIFIC R.R." with open
front and back and oval-cut windows.

28-10 "Zephyr" Locomotive and Coal Car
Maker undetermined
U.S.A., c. 1880-90
L. 12¼"

Locomotive on green base, with black boiler, stenciled in gilt
"ZEPHYR," gilt stenciled trim, red cab with two arch-cut windows on
sides and front, red smokestack, and gilt pistons with steel rods; set on
two ornate iron wheels and two tin wheels; brass and steel clockwork
beneath locomotive. Green coal car attached, with gilt stenciled trim.

28-11 "America" Locomotive
James Fallows & Co.
Philadelphia, PA, c. 1883
L. 12"

Locomotive with black tin boiler stenciled in gilt "AMERICA," orange cab with gilt trim, two arch-cut windows on each side and blue roof, gilt bell and gilt cylinders with steel pistons; set on four iron wheels; brass and steel clockwork in floor of cab.

28-12 Wooden Locomotive
D. P. Clark and Co.
Dayton, OH, c. 1900-09
L. 12¾"

Orange steam-type locomotive, 4-4-0, with black and gilt striping, headlamp with tin center, black wooden smokestack, gilt iron bell, whistle and steam ejector with black tin covers; steel piston rods, attached to back drive wheels, move in and out of wooden cylinder block; set on yellow iron wheels with flywheel on axle frame. Friction toy.

28-13 Red and Black Locomotive and Tender
D.P. Clark and Co.
Dayton, OH, c. 1900-09
L. 17¼"

Black wood steam-type locomotive, 4-4-0, with red trim, white and gilt striping, cab with square-cut window on each side and with jointed tin piston strips attached to drive wheels and moving in and out of wooden cylinder block; black iron wheels with flywheel on axle frame resting between drive wheels and vertical brass rod coupler. Black wood tender with red trim; set on four iron wheels. Friction toy.

29 | Track Trains, Non-Electric

A logical development in the design of toy trains was the addition of miniature railroad tracks. In some cases, the only major alteration necessary to the toy was to convert the wheels into a flanged variety which would fit onto the track. If the track was to be curved, another necessary change was to change the wheels from their former rectangular alignment into an arrangement which would conform to the arc of the track; this was done either by slanting stationary wheels in the earlier models or by providing pivots which would do the job.

Accuracy and standardization in manufacture were an absolute necessity if this line of development was, literally, to stay on the track. It did, and all other trains were left in the smoke.

Some track trains depended only on human energy to run (29-1), but it was clockwork trains which lent themselves most naturally to conversion to track trains, either by a mechanism fitted onto the locomotive or by a separate mechanism (see color illustration). These track models were made in the United States by most of the clockwork companies discussed in the previous section and, in addition, by several German and other European companies including Märklin, Bing, and Carette.

Live-steam trains in this country were almost invariably fitted for running on tracks, those made by Eugene Beggs of Paterson, New Jersey, and by the Weeden Manufacturing Company of New Bedford, Massachusetts, being the best examples. These trains were simply toy steam engines (see section 22) designed in train form. Their great appeal lay in the similarity of their power and operation to that of real steam trains. Compared to clockwork trains, however, they were not strong; they were also somewhat difficult to operate and could definitely be dangerous. With the advent of electric trains, which were an improvement in all of these areas, live-steam trains were outclassed.

29-O Elevated Railway Locomotive and Tender (No. 2 Gauge)
   (color plate)
Hubley Mfg. Co.
Lancaster, PA, c. 1892
L. 11¼"

Black steam-type locomotive, 2-2-0, with gilt molded ribbing, bell and steam ejector, brad-like coupler, steel piston rods connecting drive wheels to stationary rods at cylinders, steel flanged wheels, hooked iron rod suspended from whistle; black, gilt-trimmed tender. Steel and brass clockwork mechanism bolted at center of circular black iron two-rail track with four yellow and orange arches; horizontally rotating iron rod for hooking onto locomotive rod. Clockwork moves locomotive when the two hooked rods are connected.

29-1 "No. 32. New Elevated Rail Road in Circular Form"
C.C. Shepherd
New York, NY, c. 1879
L. 15"

Wooden steam-type locomotive, 4-2-0, with black paper-covered engine, purple base and cowcatcher, black and orange smokestack, black and orange lithographed papered cab with unpainted wooden roof; set on black wooden flanged wheels, front wheels pivoting; steel hook at front for pivoting steel rod; unpainted wood tender, stamped "COAL CAR"; set on four pivoting flanged wheels. Circular track, unpainted wood, elevated on eight wood pillars attached to elevated pedestal at center by wooden rods. Train moves along track with steel rod when handle is turned to rotate central disk.

29-2 Tin and Steel Locomotive
(Beggs 1⅞" Gauge)
Probably Eugene Beggs
Paterson, NJ, c. 1880
L. 13¾"

Live-steam locomotive, 2-4-0, with black tin body, red iron cowcatcher, polished tin engine cover with fenders, steel smokestack, whistle and steam ejector, black Brittania metal bell, glass end and brass cover on boiler, red and black tin cab, and die-cast cylinders with steel and brass pistons attached to drive wheels; set on red and black die-cast flanged wheels, front wheels pivoting; tubular tin kerosene lamps, with cloth works.

29-3 Locomotive with Passenger and Postal Cars (Beggs 1⅞"
Gauge)
Eugene Beggs
Paterson, NJ, c. 1885
L. 32½"

Live-steam locomotive, 2-4-0, with black tin body and headlight decorated with gilt and red striping, polished steel engine cover with fenders, bell, whistle and steam ejector, black-painted brass boiler with glass end beneath cab, and die-cast cylinders with piston rods attached to drive wheels; set on die-cast flanged wheels; black tin coal bunker attached; detachable cab cover and detachable tubular kerosene lamp with cloth wicks. Postal car and parlor car of lithographed tin and cardboard.

29-4 "No 40" Locomotive and "Twentieth Century Limited Express" Passenger Train (No. 1 Gauge)
Ives Mfg. Corp.
Bridgeport, CT, c. 1908-10
L. 41"

Black cast-iron steam-type locomotive, 4-4-0, labeled "No 40," with gilt and red trim, bell, whistle and steam ejector, steel brake rod and reverse control lever projecting from rear of cab, and steel piston strips, connected to rear drive wheels, which move in and out of cylinders; set on steel drive wheels with cast-iron spokes and on pivoting tinplate front wheels; clockwork inside steel box below engine. Black painted tin tender, labeled "T.C.L.E. No 40," with steel hook-and-brace coupler, and lithographed combination car and parlor car, each labeled "TWENTIETH CENTURY LIMITED EXPRESS," etc.

29-5 No. "20" Locomotive with Passenger Train (O Gauge)
Märklin Bros.
Goppingen, Germany, c. 1910
L. 27½"

Black tin steam-type locomotive, 0-4-0, labeled in gilt "20" and "-0-," gilt and red striping and embossed ribbing, polished aluminum steam ejector and cylinders, on nickel-plated die-cast flanged wheels; brass and steel clockwork inside engine. Black tin tender, with gilt and red lithographed detail and dual-locking steel coupler. Two passenger cars and freight car, variously lettered. Labeled with "MC" insignia.

29-6 Locomotive with Passenger Train (O Gauge)
J. A. Issmayer
Nuremberg, Germany, c. 1912
L. 4¾"

Green tin steam-type locomotive, 0-2-2, with gilt and red striping, smokestack and cab roof, gilt die-cast whistle, eye coupler, lithographed detail inside cab; clockwork inside engine; set on die-cast flanged wheels. Three passenger cars. Labeled "J.A.J."

29-7 Ives "No. 19" Track Railway Locomotive and Lithographed Freight Train (O Gauge)
Ives Mfg. Corp.
Bridgeport, CT, c. 1917-29
L. 49"

Black cast iron steam-type locomotive, 0-4-0, labeled "No. 19," with two cut windows on each side of cab and steel piston strips connected to rear drive wheels and moving in and out of black cylinders; set on steel wheels with red cast-iron spokes; clockwork within steel box beneath engine. Tender, freight car, tank car, and livestock car, with hook-and-brace couplers, variously painted, lithographed and lettered. Labeled "IVES," "THE IVES R.D.," "THE IVES MINIATURE RAILWAY SYSTEM," etc., and impressed "PAT. APR. 4, 1911 1917."

**29-8 "1835-1935" Locomotive
and Train on Circular Track
Maker undetermined
Germany, c. 1935
L. 3"**

Diminutive locomotive and train,
composed of flat tin pieces
clasped together, with steam-
type green locomotive, tender
and two parlor cars; set by strips
into slot around perimeter slot
track of circular platform containing clockwork; platform lithographed with railway scene and
labeled "1835 1935." Toy com-
memorates centennial of German
railways.

30 | Electric Trains

Electric trains have been made in such great numbers, collected so
widely, and so many works written about them that it is pointless, indeed impossible, to go into meaningful detail about them here. The
collector seriously interested in them is advised to consult the bibliography, to arrange to see some of the great collections, and to
take what follows as only a sampler.

Suffice it to say that manufacture of electric trains began in
America in the very last years of the nineteenth century. The Carlisle
and Finch Co. of Cincinnati, Ohio, manufactured its first electric
track train in 1896 and continued production until World War I. Shortly after the initial Carlisle and Finch trains, the first Lionel models appeared, as did those of several other manufacturers (such as
Howard and Knapp, both of New York, and Voltamp of Baltimore,
later Boucher, all of which ceased making electric trains by the early 1930s).

The prestigious firm of Ives & Co. made electric trains from 1910 until the company's financial failure in the early 1930s when it was
taken over by Lionel. Lionel had begun making trains for Ives in 1931;
Ives finally collapsed in 1932; there was a "Lionel-Ives" line in 1933;
and the "Ives" name was used on certain Lionel equipment through
the late 1950s. Other companies came and went. American Flyer of
Chicago and Dorfan of Newark, New Jersey, are the most notable.

A few words about locomotive classification: the frequently seen
designations of 4-4-0, 4-6-2, etc., are decipherable as follows: the
first number refers to how many wheels there are on the pilot truck at
the front of the locomotive; the second number refers to how many
driving wheels there are; and the third number refers to how many
trailing-truck wheels there are at the rear.

And a word on gauges (this applies to the previous category also): a time-honored gauge-designation developed to describe the distance between the two inside edges of the running rails of toy train tracks. The most common American gauges are listed below:

HO gauge =	½"	or 12.7 mm.
OO gauge =	¾"	or 19 mm.
S gauge =	⅞"	or 22.2 mm.
O gauge =	1¼"	or 31.8 mm.
No. 1 gauge =	1¾"	or 44.5 mm.
No. 2 gauge =	2"	or 50.8 mm.
Standard gauge =	2⅛"	or 54 mm.

30-O Lionel No. "262E" Electric Locomotive and Passenger Train (O Gauge) (color plate)
Lionel Mfg. Corp.
New York, NY, c. 1927-35
L. 42"

Steam-type, remote-control locomotive, 2-4-2, labeled "262E," with black stamped steel engine and cab, black die-cast base and cowcatcher, reverse control lever, copper railings, smokestack and steam ejectors, concealed headlight with glass cover, brass trim and bell, and steel piston rods moving in and out of black die-cast cylinders; set on steel-plated red die-cast wheels, front and rear wheels pivoting; electric motor inside engine. Black stamped-steel tender, with gilt brass and copper trim, labeled "LIONEL LINES." Baggage car, Pullman car, and observation car, each with gray stamped steel body and steel hook-and-lock couplers, detachable roof, and set on two trucks of four tinplate flanged wheels; variously labeled.

30-1 No. "171" Locomotive (No. 2 Gauge)
Carlisle and Finch Co.
Cincinnati, OH, c. 1903
L. 12"

Electric steam-type locomotive, 0-4-0, labeled in yellow relief "171." Black tin engine with polished tin-plate cover and fenders; steel steam ejector, tin-plate bell, black tin smokestack, black and silver iron headlamp labeled "171," red iron cowcatcher with black brace and green wooden base, and black tin cab with polished tin-plate roof. Set on red iron wheels with steel rims and brass piston rods which move in and out of black tin cylinders. Electric motor inside engine.

30-2 Ives No. "3218" Locomotive and Lithographed Passenger
    Train (O Gauge)
Ives Mfg. Corp.
Bridgeport, CT, c. 1910-18
L. 36½"

Electric-type black cast-iron locomotive, 0-4-0, labeled "MOTOR
3218," with red trim, headlamps, pantographs, square-cut windows
and one door on each side; set on steel wheels with red cast-iron
spokes; electric motor inside cab. Lithographed baggage car and
two parlor cars, labeled "60 EXPRESS SERVICE BAGGAGE U.S. MAIL 60"
and "62 PARLOR CAR 62," respectively, each set on two pivoting trucks
of four tin-plate flanged wheels.

30-3 Ives No. "3243 N.Y.C. & H.R." Locomotive and White Passenger
    Train (Standard Gauge)
Ives Mfg. Corp.
Bridgeport, CT, c. 1921-28
L. 67"

Electric-type locomotive, 4-4-4, rubber stamped "3243 N.Y.C. & H.R.,"
with white stamped steel body, white cast-iron base and white cast-
iron pivoting platforms with steel hook-and-brace couplers at each
end; set on die-cast wheels with red spokes; electric motor inside cab.
Buffet car, parlor car, and observation car, variously labeled. Rubber
stamped "THE IVES RAILWAY LINES" and embossed "IVES TOYS PAT. FEB.
20-12."

30-4 American Flyer No. "4678" Locomotive and "Hamiltonian"
    Passenger Train (Standard Gauge)
American Flyer Mfg. Co.
Chicago, IL, c. 1925-36
L. 61¼"

Electric-type locomotive, 0-4-0, labeled "4678," with red stamped
steel sides, maroon stamped steel roof and gray stamped steel base,
gilt window and door frames, ladders, bell, pantographs and headlights, cast-iron cowcatcher and tanks at each end, steel hook-and-
lock couplers, and brass and steel railings; set on steel-plated red die-

cast wheels; electric motor inside cab. Club car, Pullman car and observation car, each labeled "HAMILTONIAN," etc., has red stamped-steel sides and maroon stamped-steel roof, extensive gilt trim and accessories. Labeled "BUILT BY 'American Flyer' LINES," etc.

30-5 American Flyer No. "4689" Electric Locomotive and "President's Special" Passenger Train (Standard Gauge)
American Flyer Mfg. Co.
Chicago, IL, c. 1928-34
L. 93"

Electric-type remote-control locomotive, 4-4-4, labeled "4689" and "The Commander." Stamped steel body (black base, light turquoise sides, dark turquoise roof) and pivoting platforms. Cast-iron cowcatchers and tanks, brass posts, steel hook-and-lock couplers, gilt headlights with glass bulbs, gilt railings, bell and pantographs, and silver flag; set on steel-plated die-cast wheels; electric motor inside cab. Club car, Pullman car, diner car, and observation car, all labeled "PRESIDENT'S SPECIAL," etc. Each has stamped steel body designed and colored similar to locomotive with extensive gilt trim and accessories. Labeled "BUILT BY 'American Flyer' LINES."

30-6 Lionel Mfg.-Ives "No 1760-E" Locomotive (Standard Gauge)
Lionel Corp.

New York, NY, c. 1931-32
L. 84"

Steam-type remote control locomotive (Lionel No. 384E), 2-4-0, labeled "No 1760-E" with black stamped steel engine, black die-cast
base and cowcatcher with green trim, headlight with glass bulb, gilt
smokestack and steam ejectors, and steel piston rods moving in and
out of black die-cast cylinders; set on steel-plated red die-cast wheels,
front wheels pivoting. Labeled "IVES LINES" and "IVES 'STANDARD' BILD-
A-LOCO. . . ." This locomotive was made by the Lionel Corporation for
the Ives Corporation during the time when Lionel bought out Ives.

30-7 Lionel "No 400E" Blue Comet Electric Locomotive and
Passenger Train (Standard Gauge)
Lionel Mfg. Corp.
New York, NY, c. 1932
L. 74½"

Steam-type remote-control locomotive, 4-4-4, labeled "No 400E," with
turquoise-blue stamped steel engine and cab, navy-blue die-cast
base, concealed headlight with glass and copper cover, cast-iron
cowcatcher, copper railings, smokestack, steam ejectors and tanks,
trapezoidal-cut window on each side of cab, gilt detail inside cab, gilt
bell, and steel pistons moving in and out of navy-blue die-cast cylinders; set on steel-plated red die-cast wheels, front and rear wheels
pivoting; electric motor inside engine. With oil tender, passenger cars,
and observation car. This is one of the most elaborate and elegant
American electric trains made.

30-8 Lionel "No. 381E" Electric Locomotive (Standard Gauge)
Lionel Corp.
New York, NY, c. 1932
L. 5¼"

Electric-type remote-control locomotive, 4-4-4, labeled "No. 381E," with army-green stamped steel body, black stamped steel base and cowcatchers, steel hook-and-lock coupler, brass railings, gilt signal lights, grids and pantographs and gilt die-cast headlights; set on steel-plated red die-cast wheels, front and rear wheels pivoting; electric motor inside cab. Labeled "LIONEL BILD-A-LOCO," etc.

3O-9 Lionel No. "249E" Electric Locomotive and Lithographed Freight Train (O Gauge)
Lionel Corp.
New York, NY, c. 1935-41
L. 63¾"

Steam-type remote-control locomotive, 2-4-2, labeled "249E," with black stamped steel engine and cab, black die-cast base and cow-catcher, plastic lanterns, steel smokestack, bell, steam ejectors and railings, and steel piston rods moving in and out of black die-cast cylinders; set on black die-cast wheels, front and rear wheels pivoting; electric motor inside engine. Tender, freight car, cattle car, and caboose, lithographed and labeled in various colors, styles, and motifs. Labeled "LIONEL LINES," etc.

31 | Automobiles, Pull Toys and Friction Toys, Tin and Stamped Steel

The early development of the automobile coincided nicely, at the turn of the century, with the heyday of the friction toy. These toys, powered by a powerful flywheel mechanism, had originated in Germany in the 1880s, but were popularized in America mainly by several interrelated companies in the Midwest. The toys were most often made of tin with reinforcing wooden blocks to add weight and strength and with cast-iron accessories. Some of them are rather fanciful in design—one indeed doubts whether anything quite like the machine in the color illustration existed in the real world. The very nature of the friction mechanism encouraged rough play, and it is difficult today to find these toys in good condition.

Tin pull toys in automobile form appeared at about the same time, and manufacturers often simply deleted Dobbin from a horse-drawn model, added a steering mechanism and perhaps a token motor box—and voilà! (See, for instance, illustration 31-1.) Though colorful and charming, these tin pull-toy autos had the same drawbacks as the earlier tin toys—flimsiness of construction and poorly applied paint—which allowed foreign competition practically to drive many companies out of business. But to save the day came a protective tariff on foreign-made toys in the early 1920s. If one wanted to buy a fine German-made tin automobile, such as the one by Bing shown in illustration 31-6, one had to be willing to pay a price which included a government-imposed surcharge of a whopping seventy-five percent!

But Americans were not forced entirely to settle for second-rate goods. Many of the tin toys were perfectly acceptable to many buyers and the cast-iron toy automobile manufacturers were doing well (see section 32). Moreover, for the child who really wanted to play rough with toys, there was stamped steel. The Buddy "L" toys, for example, (see illustration 31-7) were virtually indestructible.

31-O Touring Automobile with Driver and Passenger (color plate)
Dayton Friction Toy Co.
Dayton, OH, c. 1910
11" x 4¼" x 5"

Touring auto with red tin body, gilt trim, two sets of back-to-back gilt tin bucket seats, simulated folded gilt tin hood, gilt tin headlight and fenders, and chartreuse tin grid; set on four gilt iron wheels, with iron flywheel resting between steel disks at back wheels. Cast-iron boy driver and girl passenger. Impressed "AP 27 09." Friction toy.

**31-1 Brougham Cab with Driver
and Passenger
D.P. Clark and Co.
Dayton, OH, c. 1900-09
11" x 3½" x 7½"**

Tin cabriolet, with black wooden sides, gilt trim, circular-cut window on each side of hood, maroon and red tin mudguards, gilt interior, and orange and black wooden elevated back driver's seat; set on orange wooden and black steel chassis on two pairs of silver cast-iron wheels, with cast-iron flywheel resting on axle. Seated cast-iron woman passenger with movable arms and pastel-blue suit and hat. Cast-iron boy driver in knickers and gilt flat hat. Friction toy.

31-2 Touring Automobile with Passengers
D.P. Clark and Co.
Dayton, OH, c. 1900-09
10¼" x 3½" x 7"

Touring auto with red tin sides, gilt trim, two gilt and red wooden seats with back rests, red wooden engine with gilt trim and headlamps, gilt and red iron steering wheel and tin pie-dish grid; set on two pairs of gilt cast-iron wheels, with cast-iron flywheel resting on axle. Four metal passengers. Friction toy.

31-3 Open-Air Car (Automobile Version)
James Fallows & Co.
Philadelphia, PA, c. 1905
7" x 4" x 5"

Black tin automobile with red high-back seat and wire steering rod; set on four gray tin wheels. Labeled "PAT JU 1887."

31-4 "Winchendon Automobile" Racer
Maker undetermined
Possibly M.E. Converse and Son
Winchendon, MA, c. 1908
9" x 4¼" x 5"

Blue auto racer, with wooden base and engine and open tin seat, seating cast-iron driver at gilt cast-iron steering wheel; set on four red cast-iron wheels. Stenciled "Winchendon" and "AUTOMOBILE."

31-5 "RK" Touring Automobile
W.E. Schieble Toy and Novelty Co.
Dayton, OH, c. 1909-20
14" x 4½" x 7½"

Touring auto, blue and gilt tin and wood, labeled "RK," with black interior, two bucket seats at front, and chauffeur in green uniform at right-hand-drive cast-iron steering wheel; set on four tin simulated tires and on two cast-iron wheels touching lead flywheel mechanism. Friction toy.

31-6 Coupe with Chauffeur
Gebrüder Bing
Nuremberg, Germany, c. 1925
8½" x 3¾" x 4½"

Deep turquoise-blue tin coupe, with black roof and fenders, cream-white trim, running board and grill, cut windshield and windows; set on four simulated white tires with orange spokes; pivoting front wheels, steel axle at front, brass casing running through wooden block with axle at rear. Chauffeur (two molded tin halves clasped together), in gray uniform, seated on right side of front seat. Labeled "Bing" and "BW GERMANY."

31-7 Black Model T "Flivver Roadster"
Buddy "L" Corp.
East Moline, IL, c. 1926
10½" x 5¼" x 7"

Black stamped-steel Model T roadster, with stamped grid, doors and trunk, and simulated convertible top; set on four red and silver cast-iron simulated tires, front tires on pivoting joint.

31-8 Black Model T "Flivver Coupe"
Buddy "L" Corp.
East Moline, IL, c. 1926
11" x 5½" x 7"

Black stamped-steel Model T coupe, with steering wheel, stamped grid, doors and trunk, two cut windows on each side; set on four red and silver cast-iron simulated tires, front tires on pivoting joint.

32 | Automobiles, Pull Toys, Cast Iron

American cast-iron toy automobiles also hit the market soon after their real-life counterparts hit the road. Though some of these horseless carriages were made by the same companies which had produced the elaborate horse-drawn cast-iron toys previously discussed, many of these companies did not manufacture automotive toys—either because they chose not to or because they went out of business. The mighty Ives Company, for instance, is known to have made only one toy car (see 33-1) and Carpenter and Pratt & Letchworth had faded into obscurity or oblivion. Dent, Wilkins (later Kingsbury), Harris, Hubley, and Kenton all adapted to the newer forms, however, and were joined by such new companies as Arcade, Kilgore, and Champion. As in earlier years, there were virtually no foreign cast-iron toys made.

The progress of real automobile design can be followed, in a rough way, by surveying the design of the toy counterparts as a glance at the illustrations shows. We go from old-fashioned "buggies" and odd-looking racing machines to recognizably almost-modern forms. Except in the cases of model cars, however, the toy companies tended to lag behind the real car companies by several years, and one cannot date a toy car with any degree of certainty by comparison with what was coming off the assembly line in any given year in the real world.

These "new" cast-iron toys generally featured much more simplified designs than their horse-drawn counterparts. Two-piece (half and half) construction was common, and usually the quality of detailing is not up to the standards of the earlier toys. There were exceptions, however, and the Packard illustrated in color is one of them. It has a realistically molded engine which is displayed when its hood is lifted; its doors open and shut; and its construction is of many pieces carefully integrated into a convincing design. Toys of this caliber, as one would expect, bring premium prices (assuming fine condition). This can be contrasted with the limousine shown in illustration 32-6 which is of the two-piece construction described above.

During the Depression years, the quality of iron automobiles declined even more with the addition to the market of more and more die-cast and slush-cast toys. Finally, the great influx of foreign imports after World War II resulted in a still further lowering of quality in design and construction.

32-0 "Packard Straight 8" Limousine with Opening Hood
(color plate)
Hubley Mfg. Co.
Lancaster, PA, c. 1928
10½" x 3¾" x 4¼"

Green and black cast-iron limousine with three cut windows on each side, opening front doors, unpainted chauffeur and wheel, silver grid, and engine displayed behind hinged green hood when opened; set on four simulated tires with spare tire at back.

32-1 Small Roadster with Steering Rod
Harris Toy Co.
Toledo, OH, c. 1903
3¾" x 2" x 3"

Red painted cast-iron roadster, with open-work seat on box-like body, pivoting steering wheel and four simulated tires.

32-2 "Peerless" Auto Racer with Driver
Probably Kenton Hardware Mfg. Co.
Kenton, OH, c. 1909
7½" x 3" x 3¾"

Silver-colored auto racer and driver, with cylindrical hollow front and seat with cut gear shift; set on four red simulated tires. Labeled in relief "PEERLESS" on both sides.

32-3 Touring Auto
Kenton Hardware Mfg. Co.
Kenton, OH, c. 1911
9" x 3" x 5¼"

Touring auto, painted white, with black roof on frame over front and back seats, gilt trim, projecting headlamps, utility boxes on both sides, two pressed doors on each side; set on four silver and yellow simulated tires; detachable steering wheel, unpainted.

32-4 "Automobile Racer" with Bucket Seats
Kingsbury Mfg. Co.
Keene, NH, c. 1911
9½" x 3¾" x 4"

Silver and gilt auto racer, with orange and green stripes, bucket seats and right-hand drive wheel; set on four rubber tires; bell between front tires with tin tab on front axle which strikes bell. Cast-iron driver dressed in blue uniform. Clockwork stamped "PATENTED."

32-5 Small Red Coupe with Spare Tire
Maker undetermined
U.S.A, c. 1925
5" x 1¾" x 2"

Red painted cast-iron coupe, with open bottom, molded grid, headlamps and spare tire, with pressed door detail on either side; set on four red simulated tires.

32-6 Limousine
Hubley Mfg. Co.
Lancaster, PA, c. 1928
6¾" x 2" x 3½"

Black cast-iron limousine, constructed of two molded halves jointed together, open-bottomed, with four cut windows on each side; set on four red simulated tires.

32-7 "Yellow Cab Co." Auto Taxicab
Arcade Mfg. Co.
Freeport, IL, c. 1928
9" x 3" x 4½"

Black and orange painted cast-iron taxicab, with wire mesh grid, arrowhead bumpers, simulated spare tire, three cut windows and two pressed doors on each side; set on four simulated orange and white tires. Labeled in relief "ARCADE MADE IN U.S.A."

32-8 No. "5 Auto Racer"
Hubley Mfg. Co.
Lancaster, PA, c. 1928
9½" x 3¾" x 4"

Cast-iron racing auto, labeled in relief "5," with red engine roof opening on both sides to reveal silver engine; black grid, silver body, with indentation for driver's seat, and driver in red costume at red wheel; set on four rubber tires. Tab of tin connected to back axle strikes spokes inside back right tire causing auto to make cracking noise when pulled. Tires impressed "HUBLEY MFG. CO. BALLOON 34X5 CORD."

32-9 Black Model T Coupe
Arcade Mfg. Co.
Freeport, IL, c. 1930
6½" x 2½" x 4"

Black Model T coupe, with open bottom, molded headlamps, pressed door and two cut windows on each side, windshield with visor, nickel-plated driver and wheel; set on four black and silver simulated tires. Impressed "ARCADE MFG. CO."

32-10 "T-100" Sportscar
Maker undetermined
U.S.A., c. 1935
10¼" x 4" x 3¾"

Green painted cast-iron sports car, with black loose-fitting fenders and running boards and nickel-plated trim; rotating steering wheel, pivoting windshield, license no. "T-100," spare tire at back and headlights at front; set on four nickel-plated simulated tires.

33 | Automobiles, Clockwork and Wind-Up Toys

The excellence of the products of the German toymaking industry is illustrated nowhere better than in the clockwork and wind-up automobiles manufactured in the first two decades of this century and again in the period between the two World Wars. As discussed in section 31, it was the cost-efficiency and design and detailing capabilities of European competition which brought on the heavy tariff on toys in the 1920s.

Particularly in the period before World War I, the contrast between American and German models is astonishing. Contrast, for instance, the meticulous detailing, elaborate accessories, and general elegance of design in the Carette model in the color illustration or the Gunthermann or Bing touring autos in illustrations 33-2 and 33-3 with the Wilkins automobile in illustration 33-4. These examples were made within two or three years of one another, and the illustrations speak for themselves. We are talking about two entirely different approaches to toy-making and one is entitled to one's preference—but in today's market, it is the German toy cars which are bringing top dollars.

Also illustrated here are examples of tin mechanical toy autos from three other European countries in the 1920s and 1930s. The French "JDEP" model (33-6) is the epitome of the Gallic virtues of refinement, elegance, and taste. The Italian Ingap model (33-8) is bursting with colorful nationalistic enthusiasm and bravura. The English Wells Rolls Royce (33-9) is sedate, proper and coolly smooth. On the basis of these three toys at least, it is hard to deny the existence of "national character."

All of these foreign toys ceased to be imported, of course, with the onset of World War II, and even before that their quality had begun to decline—for the same economic reasons which caused a similar decline in the quality of American toys. But this was little consolation for the American toy industry, for shortly thereafter it too ground to a halt to turn to war production—and it never fully returned.

33-0 Limousine with Detachable Headlamps (color plate)
Georges Carette and Co.
Nuremberg, Germany, c. 1911
16" x 5½" x 8½"

Green and black limousine, with chrome and rose-red trim and black fenders and running boards; handbrakes, opening doors with latches, chauffeur's cab, cut windows and windshield; set on four rubber tires. Lithographed chauffeur in black uniform at right-hand-drive wheel; clockwork between back tires. Detachable headlamps and side-lamps of unpainted tin with glass covers.

33-1 Roadster with Driver
Ives, Blakeslee and Williams
**   Co.**
Bridgeport, CT, c. 1898
6¼" x 3½" x 4½"

Red painted cast-iron roadster with banistered seat, steering rod, pivoting front tires and box-like body; set on four simulated tires. Clockwork beneath body. Driver, dressed in bow tie and derby.

33-2 Gilt-Trimmed Touring Auto
**   with Passengers**
S. Gunthermann
Nuremberg, Germany, c. 1903
8" x 3½" x 5¾"

White painted tin open touring auto, with gilt and black trim, brown lithographed upholstery, black fenders with steps and pivoting brake handle touching gear on back axle; set on four rubber tires, front tires on pivoting joint; seating three painted passengers —driver, man, and woman; clockwork between back tires. Labeled "ASGW" with insignia of knight with sword.

33-3 Open Touring Auto
Gebrüder Bing
Nuremberg, Germany, c. 1904
9" x 4¼" x 4¼"

Black tin touring auto, with gilt tin grids and painted gilt trim, two silver aluminum headlamps, gilt aluminum engine lamp, silver tin sidesteps, orange tin fenders, and red cast-iron simulated upholstered seats, front seats single and back seat double; set on four cast-iron wheels with rubber tires; aluminum steering wheel connected by gear joint to partially pivoting front wheels; steel and brass clockwork between back wheels.

33-4 Blue Automobile Phaeton with Woman Driver
Wilkins Toy Co.
Keene, NH, c. 1905
9¼" x 3½" x 4½"

Blue tin phaeton, with gilt trim, blue steps, gray cast-iron molded upholstery seat, gray foot rugs, cast iron right-hand-drive steering wheel, blue engine with headlamps; set on four rubber tires; wind-up mechanism between back tires. Cast-iron woman driver, dressed in red and yellow, with movable arms.

33-5 Automobile Racer with Bucket Seats
Kingsbury Mfg. Co.
Keene, NH, c. 1919
9½" x 3¾" x 4"

Silver-colored and gilded aluminum and cast-iron auto racer, with orange and green stripes, two cast-iron bucket seats, cast-iron right-hand-drive wheel; set on four rubber tires; bell between front tires with tab of tin on front axle. Clockwork revolves back axle, and tab on front axle strikes bell when toy is wound. Clockwork stamped "PATENTED."

33-6 Blue "JDEP" Open Touring Auto
Jouets de Paris
Paris, France, c. 1920
14" x 5½" x 4"

Blue tin open touring auto, with black folded hood and fenders, silver papered running boards, brown seats, black steering wheel and gear shift acting as on/off switch, two headlamps and steel horn; set on four gray simulated tires, front tires on two pivoting joints; clockwork with gear shaft beneath body. Impressed "BREVETE JDEP MADE IN FRANCE," with license no. "73 91 - JDEP."

33-7 Stutz Bearcat
Structo Mfg. Co.
Freeport, IL, c. 1920
15" x 6" x 9¼"

Base with black steel fenders over red and white cast-iron simulated tires, cast-iron steering wheel connected by gear to pivoting joints on front tires; moving brake handle connected to steel gear shaft; clockwork "engine" connected by elaborate steel gear mechanism with shaft to steel gears on back axle. Detachable sporting cover, orange stamped steel, with pressed grid, black steel windshield and seat, and red and white cast-iron simulated spare tire. Labeled in relief "STRUCTO."

33-8 "Ingap" Red and Yellow Limousine with Chauffeur
Ingap
Italy, c. 1925
11¼" x 4½" x 5"

Yellow steel limousine, with red roof and fenders, turquoise-blue trim, gilt grill with license plate "5312-PO," steel outside; set on four white simulated tires with lithographed spokes and labeled "905 x 135 SUPERFLEX INGAP." Front and back red simulated upholstered seats with chauffeur in blue livery at left-hand steering wheel behind narrow dashboard. Steel clockwork beneath rear, battery in hood; limousine rolls forward and headlamps light when clockwork is wound. Labeled "PRODOTTO ITALIANO MADE IN ITALY" with insignia map of Italy, labeled on grill and tires "INGAP," and impressed in diamond on clockwork "INGAP."

33-9 Rolls Royce Coupe
Wells
London, England, c. 1935
9" x 3" x 3¼"

Off-white lithographed tin sedan, with blue roof, fenders and running boards, black trim, silver grid and windshield, projecting trunk, covered back seat with open-cut window on each side, and chauffeur on right side of open front seat; set on four simulated tires; barrel and spring mechanism between back tires.

34 | Trucks and Vans, Tin

The story of tin trucks is similar to that of tin cars, as might be expected. Many American makers adapted to the newer forms and some did not; there was a general simplification in American toys for the sake of economy; and competition from German and other European toys was very stiff.

The lithographed tin vans are perhaps the most eye-catching toys in this category. Offset lithography had been perfected in the late nineteenth century and by the early twentieth was a widely-used process; realistic designs in many colors were mechanically rolled onto pieces of flat metal which were then cut or stamped into separate pieces and bent, folded, and molded into shape. The flat sides of toy tin vans must have seemed a perfect place to use this technique, and used they were. They appear with lithographed decorations of great variety—the most notable of which are the advertising signs, as in the van illustrated in color which bears the "Wells O'London" label.

Some toy-makers apparently used the names of well-known business concerns to promote their toys; on the other hand, many such concerns used these toys to promote business—for a price. For the tin toymakers were in the custom order business, as indeed they had also been in the horse-drawn days (see, for example, 5-15). The foreign competition was very much present in this specialty trade: illustration 34-2 shows an early German-made automotive advertising van for a Philadelphia department store. The American-made toys of this type never seem quite to catch up with their European cousins in price competition (until the toy tariff) or in design.

Workaday trucks were another matter. Sturdy tin models were turned out in great numbers: autodrays (or flat-bed trucks), "express" trucks, dump trucks, stake trucks, and moving vans. In their successful attempt to reach a "playing" audience (that is, children who would put the toys through their paces in sand, water, and what-have-you) most of the toys, however, lose some of the literal copycat quality which some of the earlier tin toys possessed. These trucks tend to be plain, relatively unornamented, almost stylized in design. They were trucks, they functioned, and that was enough. The Kingsbury Manufacturing Company (which bought out the Wilkins Toy Company of Keene, New Hampshire) made a great many toy trucks of this sort, some of which are illustrated here.

34-O No. "750 Carter Paterson Express Carriers" Delivery Van (color plate, left)
Wells
London, England, c. 1933
8½" x 3" x 4¼"

Lithographed tin van, green and black, labeled "CARTER PATERSON EXPRESS CARRIERS WE GO FAST & FAR TO SERVE YOU," with license no. "W. 1933," one articulated headlamp, opening back with windows and latch; set on four simulated tires, with driver at right-hand-drive wheel; clockwork between back wheels. Labeled "750 REGISTERED WELLS O'LONDON TRADEMARK MADE IN ENGLAND."

Blue Flat-Bed Truck with Driver (color plate, right)
Kingsbury Mfg. Co.
Keene, NH, c. 1930
9" x 3" x 4"

Blue painted tin autoray, with silver seat and open back with chain; set on four white rubber tires; clockwork between back tires. Tires impressed "KINGSBURY TOYS PAT'D KEENE N.H. U.S.A."

34-1 Red "Auto Reversing Motor Express" Truck
Wilkins Toy Co.
Keene, NH, c. 1902-11
11¼" x 3½" x 4½"

Red tin autodray, with projecting rod bumpers and gilded driver's bench; set on four rubber and yellow cast-iron tires; clockwork between back tires on pivoting joint. The Wilkins 1911 catalog states that this toy is " . . . so designed that when it meets any obstruction the motor immediately reverses and backs away until meeting another obstacle it again reverses and takes another direction, so continuing until the motor runs down."

34-2 "Strawbridge & Clothier" Delivery Van
Hans Eberl
Nuremberg, Germany, c. 1905
7½" x 3¾" x 5"

Black and red painted and lithographed tin autovan, with orange interior, labeled in gilt "80" and "STRAWBRIDGE & CLOTHIER EIGHTH & MARKET STS." with store seal, door on one side, horizontally opening back with latch; lithographed tin driver at wheel; barrel and spring mechanism between back wheels. Labeled on back "Germany" with insignia "H E N." This is an example of a custom-ordered advertising toy, this one for a Philadelphia department store.

34-3 Blue "Automobile Express" Wagon
Wilkins Toy Co.
Keene, NH, c. 1911
6¾" x 3¼" x 4¼"

Blue tin autodray, with high bench, gilt trim, and right-hand-drive steering wheel; set on four yellow cast-iron wheels; clockwork between back wheels.

34-4 Maroon "Auto Transfer" Van
Kingsbury Mfg. Co.
Keene, NH, c. 1919-30
9½" x 3¾" x 6¾"

Maroon tin autovan with open front seating cast-iron driver in orange jacket at cast-iron wheel, three diamond-shaped cut windows and open back with roof on posts; set on four silver and yellow tin wheels; clockwork between back wheels; bell between front wheels with tab on tin axle.

34-5 "Parcel Post" Van
Ferdinand Strauss
Yonkers, NY, c. 1920
10¾" x 4½" x 5½"

Orange and black lithographed tin autovan with yellow trim, labeled on both sides "PARCEL POST SPECIAL DELIVERY TRADEMARK," with driver in yellow uniform; set on four simulated tires; barrel and spring mechanism between back tires. Labeled "STRAUSS MECHANICAL TOYS KNOWN THE WORLD OVER [etc.] . . ."

34-6 "No. 10 Rapid Delivery" Van
Maker undetermined
Possibly Germany, c. 1925
7¾" x 2½" x 4"

Lithographed tin autovan, red, blue, and yellow, labeled "No. 10 RAPID DELIVERY," decorated with picture of driver and packages in screened back; set on four simulated tires; barrel and spring mechanism between back wheels.

34-7 Green "Kingsbury Motor Driven" Stake Truck
Kingsbury Mfg. Co.
Keene, NH, c. 1920
10¼" x 3¼" x 5"

Tin stake truck, painted army green, with paper label "KINGSBURY

MOTOR DRIVEN," enclosed cab and open back with stake sides; set on four white rubber tires; clockwork between back tires. Tires impressed "KINGSBURY TOYS PAT'D KEENE, N.H. U.S.A."

34-8 No. "92 E. A. Runnells Co." Delivery Van
Ferdinand Strauss
Yonkers, NY, c. 1920
9" x 4½" x 5¾"

Orange and black lithographed tin autovan, labeled "92" and on plaque in relief "E.A. RUNNELLS CO. 11 Summer St. Boston, Mass.," with two cut windows on either side and opening back door with latch; set on four pink and white simulated tires; barrel and spring mechanism between back tires. Labeled "PATENT PENDING MADE BY THE FERDI- NAND STRAUSS CORP. N.Y. U.S.A." Another custom-ordered advertis- ing toy.

34-9 "Autocar B3627" Dump Truck
Kingsbury Mfg. Co.
Keene, NH, c. 1929
14½" x 4½" x 5½"

Painted tin dump truck, labeled "Autocar" and "WHITE TRANSPORTA- TION CORP," and license no. "B3627 Mass 1928," with red cab and gray body pivoting to dump position; set on four rubber tires. Im- pressed on tires "KINGSBURY TOYS PAT'D KEENE N.H. U.S.A."

35 | Trucks and Vans, Cast Iron

American cast-iron trucks tended to be more true-to-life in design than their tin counterparts. For one thing, they were often modeled, in at least a token way, on real-life brand-name trucks—"Mack" be- ing the favorite (see color illustration). But compared to their horse- drawn predecessors, they were still simple, almost crude: fewer pieces used in the construction, less molded detail, and usually a general overall paint-job in one color with a rough stenciled label (rather than the coordinated multiple lines and relief lettering of many of the earlier cast-iron toys). But these toys were used by the twentieth-century child in rough-and-tumble play, and these con- siderations of fine design apparently made little difference; whereas a nineteenth-century child might have one horse-drawn toy with which he would play on a Sunday afternoon, the early twentieth century child of the same economic stratum would be more likely to have several with which he would play more often, in less controlled circumstances, and not necessarily on the parlor floor.

The working parts of these toys are interesting: the dump trucks actually dump (whether by a crank mechanism or by brute manual force), and the tank trucks are capable of holding liquids; the wheels roll, and so forth. Though they are heavy and sturdy, they are capable, however, of being broken and badly worn. In other words, many of them have been "played to death"; try not to acquire one of these.

As with all cast-iron toys, faking is easy and is practiced (more often on the more expensive varieties), and repainting is quite often done, especially on those working toys where paint is likely to have worn off. Needless to say, it is most desirable to acquire a cast-iron truck in mint condition—unused and in its original box if possible. But the average collector will have to settle for something less most of the time and often will be forced to settle for something in less than pristine condition, especially the rarer varieties.

35-O Mack "Gasoline" Tank Truck (color plate, left)
Arcade Mfg. Co.
Freeport, IL, c. 1932
12¾" x 4¼" x 5"

Green tank truck, with cast-iron body base stenciled "GASOLINE" and tin cylindrical gas tank set on base; set on four silver cast-iron simulated tires, back tires double. Impressed inside "ARCADE MFG. CO." and labeled outside "AN ARCADE TOY."

"Mack High Dump" Coal Truck (color plate, center)
Arcade Mfg. Co.
Freeport, IL, c. 1932
10" x 4½" x 4¼"

Red dump truck, stenciled "COAL" and impressed "Mack," with enclosed cab seating unpainted driver, crank for mechanism to raise body for dumping, and body with pivoting tailgate and tin floor; set on four rubber tires, back tires double. Impressed inside "ARCADE MFG. CO. U.S.A. 244R" and on tires "ARCADE TOYS 91-00-9."

Blue "Mack Ice" Truck (color plate, right)
Arcade Mfg. Co.
Freeport, IL, c. 1928
10½" x 4" x 4¾"

Blue truck, stenciled "ICE" and labeled in relief "Mack," with unpainted cast-iron driver, trunk with opening top, tin floor in body, and detachable tailgate; set on four rubber tires. Labeled "AN ARCADE TOY" and impressed "ARCADE MFG. CO."

35-1 Open "Coal" Dump Truck
Hubley Mfg. Co.
Lancaster, PA, c. 1928
9½" x 3¼" x 3¾"

Open red and green dump truck, labeled in relief "COAL," with molded gilt headlamps and handle and hook holding body; set on four yellow wheels. Body falls backward by gravity when handle releases hook. Labeled "It's A HUBLEY TOY."

35-2 "807 Army Motor Truck"
Hubley Mfg. Co.
Lancaster, PA, c. 1928
5" x 4½" x 5¼"

Gilded autodray, with open driver's seat, steps, headlamps, body with open back and tin floor; set on four cast-iron wheels, back wheels with springs. Impressed on plaque "ARMY MOTOR TRUCK" and "807."

35-3 Yellow "5 Ton Truck" with
**   Driver**
Hubley Mfg. Co.
Lancaster, PA, c. 1928
16½" x 5½" x 6¾"

Yellow autodray with tin floor, labeled in relief on plaques on both sides "5 TON TRUCK," with red trim, rod bumper, projecting headlamps, open-work engine, steps and low running boards; utility boxes and driver in red uniform at steering wheel; set on four red wheels.

35-4 "Mack" Dump Truck with Pulley
Arcade Mfg. Co.
Freeport, IL, c. 1928
12" x 4" x 6½"

Gray dump truck, impressed "Mack," with enclosed cab seating unpainted cast-iron driver, horizontally pivoting tailgate with latch, and
body rising on two rope pulleys attached to rod moving up and down
in spring cylinder attached to cab by thumbscrew; set on four rubber
tires, back tires double. Impressed inside "ARCADE MFG. CO." and
"223R."

35-5 "Express J & B" Truck
Hubley Mfg. Co.
Lancaster, PA, c. 1928
15" x 5" x 5"

Red open autodray, labeled in relief on plaques on both sides "EX-
PRESS J & B," with gilded headlamps, open-work steps, open-ended
body with tin floor, and detachable cast-iron steering wheel; set on
four yellow wheels, back wheels double.

35-6 Small Yellow Express Truck
Hubley Mfg. Co.
Lancaster, PA, c. 1928
4¼" x 1½" x 2¾"

Yellow express truck, open cab with roof, three molded headlamps
and open back; set on four nickel-plated simulated tires.

35-7 "Junior Supply Co" Caged Truck with Driver
Maker undetermined
Possibly Dent Hardware Co.
Fullerton, PA, c. 1930
15½" x 4½" x 7¼"

Red truck, labeled in gilt relief
"JUNIOR SUPPLY CO NEW YORK
PHILADELPHIA," with caged body
and vertically opening back
doors; set on base and cab on
four red wheels.

35-8 "Bell Telephone" Service Autovan
Maker undetermined
U.S.A., c. 1930
9½" x 3¾" x 5"

Olive-green autovan, with enclosed cab and body and open top and back. Seated cast-iron driver in cab with water keg on right side. Set on four rubber tires, back tires double. Impressed "BELL TELEPHONE" and "2011," with compartments labeled in relief "TOOLS," "KNOBS," "WIRE," "CABLE" and "SUPPLIES."

35-9 Red Autodray with Detachable Stakes
Dent Hardware Co.
Fullerton, PA, c. 1931
15¾" x 4½" x 6"

Red autodray, with gilt trim, black roof, and silver steering wheel. Detachable stakes, blue and gilt, joined through holes by chain. Set on four yellow and silver simulated tires.

36 | Construction and Farm Equipment

If trucks received hard usage at the hands of children, the same goes double for pieces of toy construction equipment. When found, they are often beat-up, the paint very worn or the metal rusted, and parts are frequently missing.

The color illustration is an exception. It is a genuine construction toy, horse-drawn at that, and practically in mint condition. Should the collector be suspicious of this toy? Well, not if he knows what it is— a "horse-drawn revival" toy of about 1940, probably made by the Kenton Hardware Mfg. Company along with a whole line of similarly "old-fashioned" cast-iron toys which continued to be made into the 1950s. It is a perfectly good and legitimate toy—but it is **late,** and this has an effect on its market value. It does illustrate the main feature of construction toys, however—their work-performance orientation. The "cement" holder tips and pours out whatever the child has put in it (hopefully not cement!).

Similarly the other toys illustrated in this section all perform the functions of their real-life prototypes to some extent—at least in the eyes of the child. Equipped with a few of these in the sand pile, a child could easily construct his own fantasy highways, bridges, and streets.

Farm toys are rather rare. Toys seem to have had an urban rather than rural audience, and it appears that relatively few were made. The McCormick-Deering tractor and thresher made by the Arcade Mfg. Company of Freeport, Illinois (36-5), is illustrative of the type. The thresher is particularly interesting, with its various moving parts, though it surely does not actually thresh. Tractors are somewhat more common, though many of the ones on the market were made after World War II.

36-O Horse-Drawn Cement Mixer with Driver (color plate)
Maker undetermined
Probably Kenton Hardware Mfg. Co.
Kenton, OH, c. 1941
14¼" x 5¾" x 6½"

Paitned and nickel-plated cast-iron wagon, with gilt trim, set on two thick red back wheels, supporting two red braces impressed "650." Nickel-plated scoop rotating on one bottom axle and attached by string pulleys to top axle; nickel-plated mixing barrel with notched rim revolving on wheel handle gear and rotating on green bottom axle. Wagon seats flat iron driver, attached by string reins to workhorse, set on nickel-plated balancing wheel.

36-1 Horse-Drawn "Contractors Dump Wagon" with Driver
Maker undetermined
U.S.A., c. 1880-1920
14" x 3¼" x 5"

Green cast-iron dump wagon, labeled in gilt relief "CONTRACTORS DUMP WAGON," with handle opening bottom to dump; set on four red wheels, front wheels pivoting; attached by shafts to black walking workhorse, with molded gilt bridle and collar; set on balancing wheel.

36-2 Cast-Iron Small "General" Steam Shovel (left)
Maker undetermined
U.S.A., c. 1910-30
5¾" x 2¼" x 4"

Nickel-plated and red-painted cast-iron steam shovel, with gilt plaques on both sides impressed "GENERAL." Open front and window-ed back, two cut doors on each side, with silhouette of worker in one door. Body on two black tractor treads, with nickel-plated semi-rotating shovel with teeth, impressed "1887."

"Panama" Steam Shovel (right)
Maker Undetermined
U.S.A., c. 1910-30
9" x 3" x 6½"

Painted cast-iron steam shovel with blue tin cab embossed "PANAMA"; profile figures in cut-out windows; silver-colored shovel on axle in arm projecting from cab, attached by chain. Shovel pivots on silver-colored tractor treads on wheels.

36-3 Cast-Iron "JAEGER" Cement Mixer
Maker undetermined
Possibly Kenton Hardware Mfg. Co.
Kenton, OH, c. 1920
6¾" x 7½" x 6"

Nickel-plated and painted cast-iron cement mixer with orange body and engine, green frame with one semi-rotating and two stationary axles, nickel-plated scoop rotating on lower stationary axle, nickel-plated cement barrel rotating on gear worked by wheel handle and set on semi-rotating axle worked by bar handle, hook hanging from second stationary axle; set on four simulated tires.
Labeled in relief ''JAEGER.''

36-4 Cast-Iron "Road Roller"
Hubley Mfg. Co.
Lancaster, PA, c. 1928
7½" x 3¼" x 5½"

Green painted cast-iron road roller, decorated with star in relief, with molded steam engine and chimney, rotating red operating wheels, and two rotating rollers at front; set on two ornate-cut wheels.

36-5 "McCormick-Deering" Tractor with Driver (left)
Arcade Mfg. Co.
Freeport, IL, c. 1928
7" x 4" x 3¼"

Gray nickel-plated and painted cast-iron tractor, labeled in relief ''McCORMICK DEERING,'' with gilt trim and detachable driver, steering wheel and seat; set on four red wheels, front wheels pivoting and back wheels with treads.

"McCormick-Deering" Thresher (right)
Arcade Mfg. Co.

Freeport, IL, c. 1928
12" x 2¾" x 4¼"

Gray cast-iron thresher, labeled in relief "McCORMICK DEERING," with red trim, projecting rotating red pulley spools and pipe, quarter-rotating tin feeder, and hook for tractor; set on four cream-colored cast-iron wheels, front wheels on pivoting joint. Labeled in relief "MADE BY ARCADE MFG. CO. FREEPORT, ILL."

36-6 Cast-Iron "Caterpillar"
Tractor With Driver
Maker undetermined
U.S.A., c. 1930
7¼" x 4½" x 5¼"

Nickel-plated and yellow painted cast-iron tractor, with tin grid impressed "DIESEL" and molded silver cast-iron engine, seating nickel-plated driver at wheel; set on four silver cast-iron wheels with rubber tread over each pair.

36-7 Crane Truck with Driver
Kingsbury Mfg. Co.
Keene, NH, c. 1930
13½" x 4½" x 8½"

Maroon tin crane truck, with gilt trim, silver seat, cast-iron driver and wheel, and tin and cast-iron frame for crane; set on four white rubber tires; clockwork between back tires. Crane is set on notched disk rotated by gear handle and has wooden spool rotated by second handle. Tires impressed "KINGSBURY TOYS PAT'D KEENE N.H. U.S.A."

36-8 Die-Cast Tractor with Driver
Maker undetermined
U.S.A., c. 1930
3" x 1¼" x 2"

Gray painted die-cast zinc alloy tractor with black engine; set on four red wheels, back wheels larger, with flat relief gray driver at driving wheel.

36-9 Weeden Steam Roller with Cab
Weeden Mfg. Co.
New Bedford, MA, c. 1935
9¾" x 4¼" x 8¼"

Live-steam-operated stamped-steel steam roller, composed of steam engine on two red and black cast-iron back wheels and gilt stamped-steel front roller in nickel-plated stamped-steel fender. Gears turn back wheels of steam roller when engine is lighted; front roller pivots manually. Embossed "WEEDEN."

37 | Fire Trucks, Automotive

The modern automotive fire truck combined into one mechanically-complicated vehicle many of the disparate functions performed by the six or seven types of classic horse-drawn fire equipment. Of course, there remained specialized vehicles, the hook and ladder truck being the most obvious. Advancing fire-fighting technology further helped to make the new automotive fire engine a complex maze of parts and equipment—and at the same time the toy industry was manufacturing products which were more simplified. The result in the toy world is a stylization of the new fire truck form, with only token attempts to mimic its details. Compared to the popularity of the "old" horse-drawn toys, it appears that the toy-buying public found the automotive type lacking in excitement, realism, and beauty—and as a result the horse-drawn type continued to be sold alongside automotive fire trucks (see, for example, 37-9).

The red Hubley hook and ladder truck illustrated in color is certainly a convincing fire truck, but more as a symbol of the prototype than as an evocation of a particular fire truck or of a moment in time. It has relatively few separate parts, relatively little detailing, and all of its accessories, except for its steel ladders, are molded into the overall cast-iron design, not separate and distinct entities. The result is a somewhat rounded, almost molten-looking form with little spatial penetration or definition. But it was bright, handsome, sturdy and relatively cheap—and that was good enough.

The other examples shown are subject to many of the above observations—later examples more so than the earlier. There is, to be sure, much to be said for the sturdy everyday play toy over the "Sunday" toy—it will stand up to active and rough play—but somehow this does not translate well onto the collector's shelf—unless, that is, the collector has nostalgic feelings for fire trucks such as these with which he may have played as a child, or wished he had. Nostalgia is a perfectly legitimate reason for collecting toys (or anything else), and, if it is automotive fire trucks that appeal to the collector, then he should follow his instincts—making sure, of course, to get the **best** fire truck possible in terms of condition, completeness, and resale value.

37-O Hook and Ladder Truck (color plate)
Hubley Mfg. Co.
Lancaster, PA, c. 1928
13" x 3" x 5¼"

Red cast-iron automotive hook and ladder truck, with molded silver headlamps, siren, molded utility chests and cylindrical seat trunk; set on four black rubber tires with tin spokes; nickel-plated ladder braces with steel ladders; steel bell with rod striking bend in back axle. Tires impressed "HUBLEY MFG. CO. BALLOON 34x5 CORD."

37-1 "Patrol" Truck
Hubley Mfg. Co.
Lancaster, PA, c. 1910
11¼" x 3½" x 5½"

Blue cast-iron automotive wagon, labeled in relief "PATROL," with molded headlight, bell, steering wheel, gilded railing with lamps, eagle decoration, utility chests, open back with perforated benches, tin floor, and tin back step; set on four copper-colored and red wheels.

37-2 Chemical "Patrol" Truck
Hubley Mfg. Co.
Lancaster, PA, c. 1910
14" x 4" x 5"

Red cast-iron autodray, carrying two steel chemical tanks and hose reel; decorated with eagle and labeled in relief "PATROL," with molded headlight, bell, seat, gilt railing, and utility chests; set on four silver and red simulated tires, front tires pivoting.

37-3 Hook and Ladder Truck
Hubley Mfg. Co.
Lancaster, PA, c. 1910
23" x 2¾" x 6"

Red cast-iron automotive hook and ladder truck, with red cast-iron engine and white trailer, with molded gilt headlight and bell, front seat and quarter-rotating back seat; decorated with gilt eagle and stars-and-stripes plaque; set on four silver and red cast-iron simulated tires; engine and trailer on pivoting joint; steel bell below front seat.

37-4 Fire Engine with Hoses
Maker undetermined
Possibly Kenton Hardware Mfg. Co.
Kenton, OH, c. 1920
12" x 3¼" x 8¼"

Red cast-iron automotive fire truck with yellow steam engine, gilded steam ejector, revolving yellow operating wheels, molded signal lamps, and cut star insignia, on four silver and yellow simulated tires.

37-5 "CFD" Fire Engine with Hose Reel
Arcade Mfg. Co.
Freeport, IL, c. 1920-30
13" x 3" x 5¾"

Red cast-iron automotive fire engine, labeled in relief "CFD," with silver bumper, grid, headlights and siren, gilt rotating hose reel, molded silver details including hose on both sides, and silver and red steam engine. Labeled in relief inside "ARCADE," and labeled outside "AN ARCADE TOY MADE IN U.S.A."

37-6 Fire Engine
Maker undetermined
U.S.A., c. 1920-35
6" x 2" x 4"

Orange cast-iron automotive fire engine, with molded headlamps, driver, hollow steam engine and back step; set on four nickel-plated simulated tires.

37-7 Open-Work Hook and Ladder Truck
Maker undetermined
U.S.A., c. 1920-35
7½" x 1¾" x 3"

Red cast-iron open-work automotive hook and ladder truck, with molded driver in helmet and two molded ladders; set on four gilded wheels.

37-8 "Chemical Truck"
Republic Tool Products Co.
Dayton, OH, c. 1925
12¼" x 4½" x 5¾"

Red painted tin automotive chemical truck, with gilt trim, flat-cut headlamps, pressed grid, tin driver and wheel, back step, and medium-sized cylindrical tank on back; four gilded tin simulated tires; enclosed friction gear mechanism on back axle. Impressed "PAT'D NOV 1-21 MADE IN U.S.A."

37-9 "Auto-Aerial Ladder Truck"
Kingsbury Mfg. Co.
Keene, NH, c. 1930
18" x 3½" x 7¾"

Automotive hook and ladder truck, with yellow-trimmed orange steel carriage, suspended rod supports for ladder, and extended yellow wooden ladder with metal rungs on spring joint and spring-and-rod shaft connected to steel plate with notches, resting on cradle. From the Kingsbury 1906 catalog, "The ladder is automatically released when the front of the truck touches a wall, desk, table leg or other obstruction, and slowly unfolds and rises to an upright position."

37-10 Hook and Ladder Truck Maker undetermined Possibly Dent Hardware Co. Fullerton, PA, c. 1931 13" x 3" x 4"

Red cast-iron automotive hook and ladder truck, with molded utility chests, signal lamps and cylindrical seat trunk; set on four simulated silver and yellow tires; bell with rod striking bend in back axle.

38 | Motorcycles

In the 1920s and 1930s toy motorcycles achieved a degree of popularity with the public, and one company, Hubley, seems to have led in their production. This category illustrates the extent to which a collector can go in collecting a series of very closely related toys of the same period, many by the same manufacturer, at affordable prices.

The interest here is in the similarity of the toys to one another, the development of a basic form, through minor variations (such as paint color) and major variations (such as the addition of an entirely new component part), to newly-worked designs. The "Indian" motorcycle shown in color is a basic model; it was available in more complex versions also—the motorcycle with side car (illustration 38-6), the "crash car" motorcycle with wagon (illustration 38-7), and the "traffic car" dray model (illustration 38-9), each more complicated than the one before. Hubley also made a Harley-Davidson series with similar variations.

These motorcycles are sturdy and well-made, though many "accessories" are simply molded into the design and the component parts are kept to the minimum necessary to carry out the design idea. The riders are realistically molded, often helmeted figures with lifelike expressions and postures which add vigor to the concept of the toy. Finally, the colors tend to be bright and snazzy, adding to the appeal. And there are many more models and colors to choose from with offbeat variations such as comic strip versions and advertising toys (see, for example, 48-11).

This is not to say that Hubley made the only toy motorcycles, but the competition does not measure up to Hubley in number of variations and availability of cycles in good condition. After World War II Hubley production swung away from the heavier and more expensive-to-make cast-iron toys to toys of die-cast zinc alloy and plastic. It is the pre-World War II toys, of course, that collectors find most appealing and exciting.

38-0 "Indian" Motorcycle (color plate)
Hubley Mfg. Co.
Lancaster, PA, c. 1925
9" x 3½" x 4½"

Yellow, silver, and gilt cast-iron motorcycle, labeled "Indian," with molded headlight, handlebars, seat, engine and back light; set on two cast-iron balancing wheels and on two rubber tires with tin spokes; tab of tin on front fender strikes spokes of front wheel. Motorcycle makes cracking noise when pulled. Labeled "It's A HUBLEY TOY."

38-1 Harley-Davidson Motorcycle
Maker undetermined
U.S.A., c. 1920
6" x 1½" x 4¼"

Unpainted cast-iron motorcycle, with molded headlight, back light, handlebars, engine, and balancing wheels; driver, dressed in knickers, jacket, and cap; set on two rubber tires with yellow tin spokes. Labeled in relief "HARLE [sic] DAVIDS [sic]."

38-2 Small "Indian Crash Car" Motorcycle
Maker undetermined
U.S.A., c. 1925
6¾" x 2¼" x 3¾"

Red cast-iron motorcycle, impressed "Indian" and "CRASH CAR," with handlebars, footrests, and engine; attached to small red wagon with railings; set on three rubber tires with tin spokes. (Possibly variation of 38-7).

38-3 "Lehmann's Motor Rad-Cycle Mars" Motorbike
E.P. Lehmann
Brandenburg, Germany, c. 1925
5" x 2¾" x 5"

Blue lithographed tin motorbike; set on three simulated rubber tires, seating rider, dressed in orange tunic and knickers, with double-jointed legs attached to pedals of front wheel; steel barrel-and-spring inside motorbike. Rider moves pedals when mechanism is wound. Impressed "LEHMANN" and "D.R.P." and with name and trademark information.

38-4 "Harley-Davidson" Motorcycle Racer
Hubley Mfg. Co.
Lancaster, PA, c. 1925
8¼" x 2½" x 4"

Blue, silver, and gilt cast-iron motorcycle, labeled "HARLEY-DAVIDSON," with molded details; set on two cast-iron balancing wheels and two rubber tires with tin spokes. Tires impressed "HUBLEY MFG. CO. BALLOON 34x5 CORD."

38-5 "Champion" Motorcycle
Champion
Geneva, OH, c. 1930
5" x 1¾" x 3¼"

Unpainted cast-iron motorcycle, with molded headlight, back light, engine, handlebars, and police driver with white painted face; set on two white rubber tires and cast-iron footrests. Labeled in relief "CHAMPION."

38-6 "Indian" Motorcycle with Side Car
Hubley Mfg. Co.
Lancaster, PA, c. 1925
9" x 3½" x 3¾"

Red and silver cast-iron motorcycle, labeled "Indian," with molded details, attached to red side car, with black bucket seat; set on three rubber tires with tin spokes. Impressed on side car "HUBLEY 1673."

38-7 "Indian Crash Car" Motorcycle with Wagon
Hubley Mfg. Co.
Lancaster, PA,. c. 1925
11½" x 5" x 5½"

Red, silver, and gilt cast-iron motorcycle, labeled "Indian" and in relief "CRASH CAR," with molded details, attached to wagon with Red Cross box, black seat and back footstep; set on three rubber tires with tin spokes, tab of tin on front fender striking spokes of front tire. Motorcycle makes cracking noise when pulled. Impressed on wagon "HUBLEY 1925."

38-8 "Harley-Davidson Parcel Post" Motorcycle Van
Hubley Mfg. Co.
Lancaster, PA, c. 1925
10" x 4" x 4½"

Olive-green, silver, and gilt cast-iron motorcycle van, labeled "HARLEY-DAVIDSON" and in relief "PARCEL POST" and "US," with molded details, attached to olive-green van, with opening back door and two cut windows; set on three rubber tires with tin spokes. Impressed on van "HUBLEY 1741."

38-9 "Indian Traffic Car" Motorcycle with Dray
Hubley Mfg. Co.
Lancaster, PA, c. 1925
11½" x 5" x 4½"

Red, silver, and gilt cast-iron motorcycle, labeled "Indian," with molded details, attached to blue cast-iron dray, labeled in relief "TRAFFIC CAR"; set on three rubber tires with tin spokes, tab of tin on front fender striking spokes of front wheel. Motorcycle makes cracking noise when pulled. Impressed on dray "HUBLEY 1922."

39 | Airplanes

The European manufacturers, especially the Germans, made many of the pre-World War I airplanes for the American toy market and these, of course, were mainly of tin. Many of these early airplanes were rather simple in design and employed offset lithography and other techniques which have been previously discussed. Some American tin toy planes were also introduced.

By the 1920s, however, the American cast-iron toy manufacturers were in the airplane market in a big way. Understandably, there was little demand from America for German airplanes during or after World War I, and the timing and the materials were just right for American industry to capitalize on the flying boom of the 1920s. Particularly after Lindbergh's trans-Atlantic flight in 1927, airplanes were the toy. The color illustration as well as illustration 39-6 demonstrate the toy industry's response to Lindy-mania as does the "Spirit of St. Louis" plane illustrated in section 47.

The use of cast iron in the "America" airplane is well handled, particularly in the detailed design of the three black and nickel-plated motors with revolving propellers. This is a toy made with attention to design and detail reminiscent of the earlier cast-iron toys. Although its weight makes iron about the last material one would think of using extensively in a real airplane, it is certainly convincingly used here.

The above is not to say, however, that German toy airplanes did not continue to be made. They did, and in great quantity.

39-O "America" Tri-Motor Airplane (color plate)
Hubley Mfg. Co.
Lancaster, PA, c. 1928
13½" x 16½" x 5½"

Gray cast-iron airplane, labeled in relief "AMERICA," decorated with red stars and star-in-circle insignia; three black and nickel-plated motors with revolving propellers attached by wire springs to pulley wheels connected to front axles; set on one small and two large rubber tires. Plane makes cracking noise (tin tab mechanism) and propellers revolve when toy is pulled. Tires impressed "HUBLEY MFG. CO. BALLOON 34x5 CORD."

39-1 Airplane with Passengers
Maker undetermined
Possibly Germany, c. 1910
10½" x 9¼" x 3½"

Yellow and orange painted tin biplane, with red trim and rotating cardboard propeller, containing two lithographed tin passengers, a driver and a woman dressed in motoring costume with umbrella; clockwork beneath seat.

39-2 White and Blue-Striped Airplane
Maker undetermined
Possibly Germany, c. 1910
8½" x 7" x 4"

Tin biplane, with white and blue-striped tin double main-wing and tail-wing connected by parallel steel rods; propeller connected to clockwork in open case beneath wings; seated man (molded tin halves clasped together), in red jacket and white cap and pants, with hands on steel reins connected to tail-wing. Propeller rotates when clockwork is wound.

39-3 Glider
Maker undetermined
Possibly Germany, c. 1910
10½" x 6¾" x 2¼"

Tin glider consisting of red-tipped white wings on steel rod frame with silver-colored plate at front and white rudder and tail at rear; small figure of pilot (lithographed tin halves clasped together) seated in recessed section between wings.

39-4 Yellow "Air Mail" Airplane
Kenton Hardware Mfg. Co.
Kenton, OH, c. 1920
7½" x 7" x 3"

Yellow nickel-plated and painted cast-iron airplane, labeled in relief "AIR MAIL," with gilded tail, four cut windows on each side and revolving propeller; set on three nickel-plated wheels. Labeled in relief "KENTON TOYS KENTON OHIO" and impressed "671½".

39-5 "D9340" Twin-Motor Airplane
Maker undetermined
Possibly Germany, c. 1920
13" x 16" x 16½"

Painted steel and tin airplane, labeled "D9340" on body and wings, with orange-brown tin body, black painted windows, hinged silver tin tail-wing decorated with black bird in circle, and silver tin wings with small pontoons at each end; twin motors with brown simulated wooden tin propellers set on steel rod braces above wings; clockwork inside box beneath motors connected to propellers by gear mechanism; set on two silver tin front wheels and silver tin balancing wheel. Airplane rolls forward and propellers rotate when clockwork is wound.

39-6 "Lindy" Airplane (left)
Hubley Mfg. Co.
Lancaster, PA, c. 1928
9½" x 10" x 3½"

Blue cast-iron airplane, with one cut window on each side and black engine with nickel-plated revolving propeller; set on two nickel-plated simulated tires and one rubber tire. Back tire attached to propeller by gear and gear shaft; propeller spins when toy is pulled. Labeled in relief "LIN-DY" and "NX21 RYAN NYP."

Small "Lindy" Airplane (right)
Hubley Mfg. Co.
Lancaster, PA, c. 1928
4½" x 3½" x 1¾"

Blue cast-iron airplane, with hole for cockpit, nickel-plated engine with revolving propeller; set on two nickel-plated simulated tires. Labeled in relief "LINDY."

39-7 "TAT" Tri-Motor Airplane
Kilgore Mfg. Co.
Westerville, OH, c. 1929
11" x 13½" x 3½"

Cast-iron airplane, labeled in relief "TAT" with arrow insignia, with blue cockpit and body and yellow wings and tail and three nickel-plated motors with revolving propellers; set on two nickel-plated wheels and blue balancing tab. Impressed "T.A.T.101.1" and labeled in relief "KILGORE."

39-8 Biplane with Revolving
       Propeller
Kingsbury Mfg. Co.
Keene, NH, c. 1930
16" x 12" x 5¼"

Gray painted tin biplane, with red, white, and blue concentric emblems, wire frame for pulling, and two rubber tires on either side of wind-up mechanism; revolving propeller connected to wooden back wheel by rod, wooden spool in tail, and rubber band.

39-9 "Lucky Boy" Tri-Motor Airplane
Dent Hardware Co.
Fullerton, PA, c. 1931
7½" x 7½" x 2"

Red cast-iron airplane, labeled in relief "LUCKY BOY" and decorated with star-in-circle insignia; three nickel-plated motors with revolving propellers; set on two red simulated tires.

39-10 Gray Airplane "52 24" Decorated with German Crosses, Mickey Mouse, and Swastikas
Maker undetermined
Possibly Germany, c. 1935
10" x 4¼" x 3"

Lithographed gray, blue, and black tin airplane, labeled "52 25," decorated with swastikas (on tail) and Mickey Mouse (near nose) with lithographed cockpit and two unpainted rotating propellers; set on three simulated tires, back tire on pivoting joint. Clockwork in cockpit is attached to wheels and propellers by a series of gears and springs. Clockwork impressed "PW."

40 | Dirigibles and Balloons

Balloons, of course, had preceded airplanes in development, and they and their successors—the dirigibles (or airships or blimps)—competed with airplanes for their place in the sky during the early years of this century.

The French seem to have been the balloonists **par excellence**, and two French balloon toys are featured here (40-1, 40-2). As one expects in French toys, the designs are complex, elegant and stylish —and with a certain Gallic touch of humor. The Germans were also in the balloon toy market—witness Lehmann's characteristically zany "Lu Na" toy (40-3).

The American dirigibles illustrated here are all cast-iron models, though some cheap tin models were also made, notably by Louis Marx & Co. The cast iron was often painted to resemble aluminum in an attempt to reduce its heavy look. If cast iron seems a bit inappropriate for airplanes, it is even more so for "lighter-than-air" craft. Typically, these toys were extremely simple in design—basically two cast-iron halves joined together and set on wheels. Interestingly, the American toys often emulated the great German prototypes, especially the "Graf Zeppelin" (40-8).

At the same time the Germans were also producing dirigible toys, of course, and Lehmann just as predictably featured them in its line (40-5). A word should be said somewhere—and it might as well be here—about the inventiveness and marketing sense of the E. P. Lehmann Patentwerke of Brandenburg, Germany. From the 1880s on, this concern produced many small tin toys, mostly lithographed and clockwork powered, which were clever, durable, and relatively inexpensive. For almost every design prototype discussed in this volume, Lehmann made a version. It was this type of German toy, among others, which was the bane of American toy manufacturers. But by the same token, these toys were the delight of millions of children and of the toy-buying public—and are highly collectible today.

40-0 "Los Angeles" Dirigible (color plate)
Dent Hardware Co.
Fullerton, PA, c. 1931
12¼" x 2½" x 4½"

Fluted cast-iron dirigible pull toy painted to resemble aluminum, cut windows and open-work underslung carriage; set on two simulated tires and one wheel. Red star-in-circle insignia, labeled "LOS ANGELES" in relief.

40-1 Aeronautic Balloon with Passengers
Maker undetermined
Possibly France, c. 1880-1900
4" x 4" x 7½"

Tin balloon, painted green, orange, and white; set on vertical steel pole inserted through bowl-shaped craft into hole in square tin stand, containing three plaster passengers; balloon turned by iron cogwheels beneath craft attached to iron pulley wheel on side.

40-2 Balloonist with Waving Arms
Maker undetermined
Possibly France, c. 1890
6½" x 3" x 9¾"

Doll figure of balloonist, half-figure with bisque head; set on cardboard torso with waving wooden arms and dressed in brown felt jacket and red fabric bow tie; each hand holding printed fabric American flag; doll set in straw basket with four vertically curved rods supporting yellow cardboard balloon with gilt band and red wooden base; string through balloon attached to wooden pulley wheel on spring behind doll. Balloonist waves flags when string is drawn out and released. Head incised "3/0."

40-3 "Lu Na" Balloon
E.P. Lehmann
Brandenburg, Germany, c. 1910
Diam. 3", H. 6"

Yellow and red lithographed tin aeronautical balloon, made of two half globes clasped together; connected by rods to metallic red basket containing passenger with movable arms, holding paper flag; string with tin loops at either end strung through basket and balloon. Balloon ascends and passenger raises flag when string is pulled taut. Labeled "LEHMANN LU NA MARKE No. 400 D.R. PATENT ENGL. PATENT MADE IN GERMANY."

40-4 Suspended Mechanical Dirigible
Maker undetermined
Germany, c. 1910
11" x 3½" x 3½"

Molded tin aircraft, painted brown, with suspended seats and revolving propeller. Hung from hook on stand.

40-5 "EPL. II" Dirigible
E.P. Lehmann
Brandenburg, Germany, c. 1910
10" x 3¼" x 3¾"

Lithographed tin and steel dirigible wind-up toy with one large and two small revolving propellers and two revolving devices at front, suspended seats, movable rudder, steel barrel and spring mechanism. Labeled "EPL. II 652 MARKE LEHMANN MADE IN GERMANY D.R. PATENTE D.R.G.M. D.R.P. ENGL. PATENTS BTE. S.G.D.G. LA FR. DEUTSCH VORAN"

40-6 Zeppelin Crackler
Maker undetermined
Possibly France or Germany, c. 1920
4¾" x 1¾" x 3"

Gilded and painted tin penny whistle toy connected at mechanism to gilt zeppelin, with whistle reed, seat and rotating propeller.

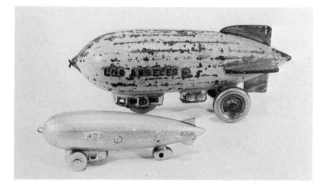

40-7 Small "Los Angeles" Dirigible (right)
Maker undetermined
U.S.A., c. 1925
7¾" x 1¼" x 3"

Nickel-plated and painted cast-iron dirigible, fluted design, with gilt tail, two underslung carriages, one open-work and one solid; set on three nickel-plated simulated tires.

"Zep" Dirigible (left)
Dent Hardware Co.
Fullerton, PA, c. 1931
5" x 1¼" x 1½"

Aluminum-colored fluted cast-iron dirigible pull toy, decorated with star-in-circle insignia; two underslung carriages set on two simulated tires. Labeled "ZEP" in relief. Part of Dent "Airport" set.

40-8 "Graf Zeppelin"
Maker undetermined
U.S.A., c. 1930
14" x 3¾" x 4"

Pastel-blue fluted cast-iron dirigible pull toy with gilt tail, three open-work carriages, two on each side and one under body; set on three nickel-plated tires. Labeled "GRAF ZEPPELIN" in relief.

41 | Boats and Ships, Pull Toys

Pull toy versions of boats, whether tin, cast iron, or other materials, are almost invariably American-made. European boats are usually of the mechanized variety (see section 42) and they are predominantly floating models. Also typically American are the riverboat and showbat forms, although there were certain of these made in Europe for the American market.

Tin pull-toy boats, as one might expect, resemble the tin toys previously discussed in construction technique and style of decoration: their basic shapes are rather simple tin forms with embellishments, often exaggerated, also made of tin; the painting is characteristically composed of one coat of thin paint with perhaps stenciling in another color and/or gilding; and imaginative names of the vessels appear with great frequency in large and fancy letters (see, for example, illustration 41-1). These toys often are set on iron wheels and axles and may have other iron or steel features added.

Cast-iron pull-toy boats, as again would be expected, have more detailing and three-dimensionality in their designs and also tend to have more moving features than their tin counterparts. There is sometimes a walking beam which moves up and down when the boat is pulled, and often the wheels and axle are arranged so as to give the toy a realistic rocking motion, an illusion of bobbing on the waves. Both riverboat and battleship themes were popular.

Finally, there are the pull toys which simulate rowing (41-4), where the action of pulling the toy across the floor activates a mechanism which causes the oarsmen to pull their oars in a fairly convincing way.

41-O "City of New York" Steam Riverboat (color plate)
Harris Toy Co.
Toledo, OH, c. 1903
15¼" x 3¼" x 5¼"

Cast-iron steamboat, with white base, perforated portholes, green and red trim, white deck with yellow-roofed tier supporting captain's cockpit with red roof, gilt whistle, black smokestack, and white life-boat. Partly rotating walking beam attached by rod to bend in wheel axle which connects two red wheels beneath fenders; boat also set off-center on balancing wheel at bow; toy sways up and down and walking beam jerks up and down when boat is pulled. Labeled in black "CITY OF NEW YORK." [Note: It is possible that this boat was manufactured by the Wilkins Toy Co. and that Harris added the "City of New York" label and then merchandised it.]

41-1 "Niagara" Steamboat
Maker undetermined
U.S.A., c. 1880
20" x 4¾" x 7¼"

White painted tin steamboat, stenciled in gilt "NIAGARA," with cylindrical pilot house, black smokestack with bell, steel staffs at either end and long narrow passengers' cabin with orange roof and gilt stenciled windows; set on two large iron wheels with orange and blue fenders and on balancing wheel at stern.

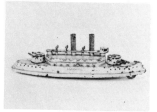

41-2 "Kearsarge" Steam Battle-ship with Detachable Gun Turrets
Maker undetermined
U.S.A., c. 1880-1920
14" x 3¼" x 4½"

White cast-iron steam battleship, with yellow decks and orange striping; tier with projecting side guns, captain's cockpit with windows, two orange smokestacks, three lights, and two holes for turrets; set on two central wheels and off-center on balancing wheel at bow. Boat sways up and down when pulled. Labeled "KEAR-SARGE."

41-3 Small Silver Steam Battle-ship with Pivoting Flagstaff
Maker undetermined
U.S.A., c. 1880-1920
6¼" x 2" x 3¾"

Silver-colored cast-iron steam battleship, with gun turrets at bow and stern, tier with smokestack and high pivoting flagstaff, guns projecting from both sides of bow; set on two pairs of small wheels.

41-4 "The Eight Oar Marine Crew"
U.S. Hardware Co.
New Haven, CT, c. 1900
14½" x 3¾" x 4¼"

Green cast-iron scull with tangerine-colored covering; set on four ornate flat coral-colored iron wheels; flat iron seated coxswain and eight tandem oarsmen in blue uniforms with sailor's hats. Each oarsman is attached to another hand-to-back, to a long yellow steel oar, and to an iron strip along inside of boat which in turn is connected to loop in axle. Oarsmen move back and forth, pulling oars in unison, when toy is pulled. Labeled in relief "PATENTED MAY. 3. 1898."

41-5 White "Showboat"
Arcade Mfg. Co.
Freeport, IL, c. 1915
10½" x 2¾" x 4¼"

White cast-iron riverboat, with green base and gilt perforated trim, tin floor and red three-quarter length tin roof, captains' turret with windows and gilt roof at top, and cast-iron stairs to roof inside; set on four gilt iron wheels; steel bell in front of back wheel axle with suspended iron clapper. Labeled "AN ARCADE TOY" and in relief "ARCADE."

41-6 Silver-Colored Battleship with Two Stacks
Maker undetermined
U.S.A., c. 1920-40
7" x 3" x 3"

Silver-colored battleship, with turrets and smokestacks, and identical bow and stern; set on two pairs of wheels. Detachable guns.

42 | Boats and Ships, Clockwork and Live-Steam Toys

Mechanical boats are the apples of the toy-boat collector's eye—especially the elaborate European ones which actually float and propel themselves through the water by means of clockwork or steam mechanisms. There are also desirable American mechanical boats, especially some of the steam models, but in general these were not made as durably as the European toys.

The color illustration gives a good idea of the appeal of the European mechanical floating boats, particularly the German ones. In addition to Carette, Märklin and Bing also made beautifully designed, elegantly detailed, and well-finished products—and on a scale which until the advent of electric trains was the most elaborate of any production toy commonly on the market. These toys were expensive when made and are now even more expensive. The usual cautions concerning rare and elaborate toys apply—watch out for repainting, added or replaced accessories, and some outright fakes. There are recent books on the subject which will be of help.

American mechanical boats tend to fall into three categories: pull toys with clockwork or other mechanisms added to propel the toys across the floor (42-1), simple steam-powered models (42-3), and, finally, attempts to outbid the European makers of the elaborate floating palaces described above. Except for the charm of the tin and cast-iron riverboat types (also seen in the pull-toy models), the American attempts simply failed to outclass the European competition where much more attention was paid to detailing or design and construction. The Germans, in particular, took great pains to make their boats watertight, to finish them with paint which was unlikely to peel in water, and in general to make them seaworthy. The higher cost of labor in America and the mass-production character of the toy industry here prevented the manufacture on a large scale of models which were aesthetically and economically competitive.

42-O Ferryboat with Cabin and Life-Boats (color plate)
Maker undetermined
Possibly Georges Carette
Nuremberg, Germany, c. 1910
14½" x 4½" x 8½"

Red and white painted tin ferryboat, with two-tiered cabin, four smokestacks, two flagstaffs, two hanging orange lifeboats, lookout deck and pivoting rudder attached to stand at stern; steel clockwork inside boat base, attached to three-bladed propeller. Boat navigates when clockwork is wound through second smokestack.

42-1 "Electra" Steamboat
Maker undetermined
Possibly George W. Brown Co.
Forestville, CT, c. 1856-70
16" x 4" x 6"

White painted tin steamboat, with

red and gilt stenciling, labeled "ELECTRA," with black twin smokestacks, steel flagstaff at stern with U.S. flag, gingerbread trim at bow, cylindrical pilot house with pagoda roof, oscillating walking beam, and red stenciled windows around cabin with red roof; set on two large cast-iron wheels with fenders and on pair of balancing wheels projecting from stern; brass and steel clockwork between wheels.

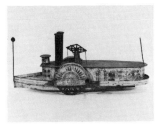

42-2 "Union" Steamboat
George W. Brown Co.
Forestville, CT, c. 1856-70
14½" x 4" x 6"

White painted tin steamboat, with gilt, green, and red stenciling, labeled "UNION," with black twin smokestacks with gilt tin bell, steel staffs at either end, cylindrical pilot house and jointed walking beam; set on two large iron wheels with fenders and on balancing wheel at stern; brass and steel clockwork between wheels. Boat moves forward and walking beam oscillates when clockwork is wound.

42-3 Brass Steamboat
Buckman Mfg. Co.
New York, NY, c. 1880
9½" x 3" x 4"

Live-steam propeller-driven steamboat, brass-plated metal, rudder with rod handle and propeller at stern; brass cylindrical boiler connected by brass tube to lead plate with lead piston moving lead wheel connected by horizontal rod to propeller.

42-4 "Atlanta" Steam Boat
Jean Schoenner
Nuremberg, Germany, c. 1900
18½" x 3¼" x 6"

Live-steam propeller-driven steam boat, labeled "Atlanta," of copper-colored tin with gray and orange trim, gray simulated plank decks, copper-colored and orange rudder with rod handle and black steel propeller at stern; gilt-striped gray tin boiler with copper smokestack at center, connected by copper tube to copper piston moving steel wheel connected by horizontal rod to propeller.

42-5 Gray Submarine with Gilt Railings
Maker undetermined
Possibly Gebrüder Bing
Nuremberg, Germany, c. 1910
10¼" x 2¾" x 3¾"

Gray tin submarine decorated with black and gilt trim, with gilt wire railings, white tin outlook cabin, black steel flagstaff and rotating gray steel propeller; clockwork inside ship, wound through cabin.

42-6 Narrow Long Boat with Eight Oarsmen and Coxswain
Maker undetermined
Germany, c. 1910
29¼" x 5" x 4"

Lithographed tin longboat, yellow-brown simulated wood, with deck containing eight oarsmen (molded halves clasped together) with flat-cut legs and blue and white costumes and with orange wooden oars set into oarlocks; oarsmen attached to one another below axle at base of each torso by horizontal steel rod running along inside of boat. Boat set on two gray tin wheels at stern and one supporting wheel at bow; steel clockwork beneath stern. Oarsmen lean back and forth at waists to pull oars when clockwork is wound. Stamped "Germany."

42-7 Live-Steam Gunboat
Maker undetermined
Possibly Gebrüder Bing
Nuremberg, Germany, c. 1905
24½" x 6" x 13"

Gray tin warship with red trim, white portholes, and applied wire and solder railings; numerous separately fashioned and applied accessories, including life-

boats, flags, ladders, smokestacks, and movable guns in turrets. Superstructure lifts off when
rigging is unhooked for access to
live-steam mechanism which
drives propeller.

42-8 "Sally" Ferry Boat
Ives Mfg. Corp.
Bridgeport, CT, c. 1920
10¾" x 3" x 5¼"

Maroon and white painted tin
ferry boat, labeled in black "SAL-
LY," with mustard-colored deck,
tent at bow deck, maroon passenger cabin with white roof, brown
smokestack, brown horn, white tin
canopy covering stern deck, and
maroon steering wheel, rudder,
and propeller; clockwork inside
boat, wound through smokestack. Stamped "IVES TOYS."

43 | Cap Guns and Exploders

Three distinct types of collectible toy are grouped here: cap pistols
which resemble real-life guns; novelty cap pistols; and cap bombs.
All are generally made from cast iron, and they tend to be rather
simple in construction and diminutive in size.

Simple cap pistols (revolvers, derringers, etc.) and cap rifles are
familiar items. They consist of a stationary body, a breech for plac-
ing an explosive cap (or in certain of them, a roll of caps) and a hammer, activated by a trigger and spring mechanism, which explodes
the cap.

Novelty cap pistols are rarer and much more expensive. These
can be divided into two types, the "head" pistols, where the head of
a man or animal forms the breech, the cap normally being placed in
the figure's mouth, and the animated pistols where a pictorial action

takes place along with the explosion of the cap. In this latter type, the variety and complexity of action is truly astounding. The prices obtained reflect this, and this type of pistol is by far the most sought-after by collectors.

Finally, there is the cap bomb, usually in the shape of a head with a ring on top fitted to a separate mouthpiece which moves up and down and often extends through the top of the head. A cap is placed between the two pieces, and it is exploded when the bomb is dropped. This type of toy was very popular at the 1876 Centennial celebration (see 47-2) and into the early twentieth century. Bombs were made in a great variety of forms, several of which are illustrated here.

Fake cap pistols, especially the expensive novelty type, are known. These are detectable in the same manner as any other cast-iron toy: by an examination of the casting for an uneven finish with indistinct detail, by discovering parts which do not fit together well, by detection of a "too-new" finish without patina, but best of all by a comparison with other truly old toys for size, general form, and overall feel.

43-O "White Cap" Revolver (color plate, upper left)
J. and E. Stevens Co.
Cromwell, CT, c. 1890
L. 7¼"

Single action, single shot nickel-plated cast-iron revolver, labeled "White Cap" in relief, with trigger, hammer, stationary cylinder and simulated chambers, decorated in relief with scrollwork and geometric designs. Impressed "PAT JUNE 17 1890."

"Best Butter" Novelty Pistol (color plate, right)
Maker undetermined
U.S.A., c. 1885
L. 5½"

Cast-iron cap pistol, labeled in relief "BEST BUTTER," single action, single shot, with two billy goats, one as hammer and the other as anvil; when trigger is pulled, the first strikes cap placed on second.

Devil's Head Cap Bomb (color plate, lower left)
Maker undetermined
U.S.A., c. 1870-1900
L. 2¼"

Cast-iron cap bomb, single shot, in shape of devil's head; cap is inserted between two parts of bomb, in mouth, and is fired by striking on hard surface.

43-1 "Johnnie's Little Gun" Cap Rifle

Ives, Blakeslee and Co.
Bridgeport, CT, c. 1888
L. 11"

Varnished cast-iron cap rifle, labeled in relief "JOHNNIE'S LITTLE GUN," single action, single shot, with trigger and hammer, trigger guard, picture in relief on both sides and decorated in relief on stock with diamond cross-hatching and on handle with row of scrollwork. Labeled in relief "PAT. FEB. 14. 88."

43-2 "Acorn" Derringer (left)
J. and E. Stevens Co.
Cromwell, CT, c. 1890
L. 3½"

Cast-iron cap derringer, labeled in relief "ACORN," single action, single shot, with partly fluted barrel, trigger and hammer, and incised with vine on partly openwork handle. Labeled in relief "PAT MAR 22 JUN 17 9 USA."

"Bomb" Derringer (right)
Maker undetermined
U.S.A., c. 1870-1900
L. 4¼"

Cast-iron cap derringer, labeled in relief "BOMB," single action, single shot, with trigger and hammer, rectangular barrel, and decorated in relief with half-moon and exploding cannon ball on handle and stock.

43-3 "The Chinese Must Go"
   Novelty Pistol
Ives, Blakeslee and Co.
Bridgeport, CT, c. 1879
L. 4¾"

Cast-iron cap pistol, labeled in relief "THE CHINESE MUST GO," single action, single shot, with figures of two men, one a white man who "kicks" the other, an Oriental, to fire cap in mouth. Labeled in relief "PAT SEP 2. 79."

43-4 "Just Out" Chicken Novelty
   Pistol
Ives, Blakeslee and Co.
Bridgeport, CT, c. 1884
L. 5¾"

Cast-iron cap pistol, labeled in relief "JUST OUT," single action, single shot; egg form at muzzle

opens to reveal baby chick when
"pecked" by figure of rooster, firing cap.

43-5 "Punch and Judy" Novelty Pistol
Ives, Blakeslee and Co.
Bridgeport, CT, c. 1880
L. 5¼"

Cast-iron cap pistol, labeled in relief "PUNCH AND JUDY," single action, single shot; Punch strikes Judy and fires cap placed on her back.
Labeled in relief "PATENTED."

43-6 Dog's Head Cap Bomb (left)
Ives, Blakeslee and Co.
Bridgeport, CT, c. 1880
L. 2"

Copper-plated cast-iron cap bomb, single shot, representing setter's
head with mouth opening for cap on flat steel spring. Labeled in relief
"PAT APR'L 23.78."

Old Man's Head Cap Bomb (right)
Maker undetermined
U.S.A., c. 1870-1900
L. 1½"

Nickel-plated cast-iron cap bomb, single shot, in shape of bearded
man's head, made up of upper and lower halves held together by
spring along vertical groove from neck over temples and head; hook
at top of head.

44 | Artillery Toys

This section will touch only very lightly on the wide collecting area of military toys. Toy soldiers are, of course, a specialty of their own on which whole works have been written and are intentionally omitted here. Other military toys (for example, battleships and planes) appear in other categories.

Nineteenth-century horse-drawn wheeled toys included a certain number of military models, especially artillery carriages. Two models of the 1880s and 1890s, one Pratt & Letchworth and one Ives, are illustrated (44-1, 44-2). Both convey the pomp and excitement of artillery parades. These, of course, are cast-iron toys of the "old" variety, with numerous parts, high-relief detailed castings, careful painting, and evidence of lavish care in design and construction. Contrast these with the 1920 "tank cannon" (44-6), where number of parts, detailing, and painting have all been reduced to the bare essentials.

The cannons featured here are all working models, and one wonders how many children shot or burned themselves or their playmates. Some of them fire rolls of relatively harmless caps and some are made for special "bangsite" toy gun ammunition, but others are made for the insertion of firecrackers while others still are, plain-and-simply, guns—using cartridges or shot. It is not recommended that these be operated today—at least without careful inspection, cleaning, and instruction—and you may need a license to operate the more lethal of them!

These cannons bring into a different focus the educational "initiation into manhood" function which many earlier toys were thought to perform. Boys had to learn to use guns at some point, and what better place to start than with an attractive, relatively harmless "toy" gun. Perhaps as a result, these cannons are rather "serious" in design, giving the impression of being truthful copies of the real thing. The concern for safety aside, they are not unattractive and are an important type of collectible toy.

44-0 Artillery Field Cannon (color plate)
Conestoga Corp.
Bethlehem, PA, c. 1925
17¾" x 4¾" x 5¼"

Army green cannon, cast-iron stock and steel barrel set on steel support on two red iron wheels, with brass buttons on support, stock and barrel, tin guard between breech and barrel, open slot at breech, and opening ammunition case on stock. Made for "bangsite" ammunition. Impressed "NO 10FC" and "NO 10CC CHARGER NO 10FC AND NO 10AC KEEP CLOSED."

**44-1 Tandem Horse-Drawn
    Artillery Carriage with
    Grenadiers
Pratt & Letchworth
Buffalo, NY, c. 1892
L. 34"**

Two pairs of animated galloping
horses pulling cast-iron wagon
carrying black cannon with brass-
finialed piston rod moving in and
out of breech, quarter-rotating on
black frame with attenuated tail,
simulated hobnails; set on two
large green and coral-colored
wheels. Four grenadiers, one with
folded arms.

**44-3 "Monarch" Cartridge
    Cannon on Four Wheels
Maker undetermined
U.S.A., c. 1880-1920
9½" x 3" x 4"**

Cast-iron cannon for firing blank
cartridges, labeled in silver relief
"MONARCH," with stationary
black barrel on red platform decorated with silver star and striping
and set on four small wheels; barrel hollow with hole in breech for
loading and hammer and trigger
set on flat steel spring in stand.

**44-2 Horse-Drawn Artillery
    Carriage with Cannon
Ives, Blakeslee and Williams Co.
Bridgeport, CT, c. 1893
L. 23½"**

Cast-iron carriage, pulled by pair
of Ives "Type II" horses, carrying
brass cannon, decorated on
stock with star in relief, with
soldered breech cover and projecting rod at muzzle; quarter-
rotating on black and gilt-
trimmed frame with attenuated
rear support with hook; set on two
coral-colored slightly concave
wheels.

**44-4 "No 1 Giant Cannon"
Maker undetermined
U.S.A., c. 1880-1920
2¾" x 1½" x 2"**

Black cast-iron cannon with bul-
bous stationary barrel set on trap-
ezoidal stand. Barrel is hollow with
hole at rear for igniting firecracker. Labeled in relief "NO 1 GIANT
CANNON."

44-5 "Anti-Aircraft Rapid Fire Machine Gun"
Grey Iron Casting Co.
Mt. Joy, PA, c. 1920
8½" x 3½" x 5¾"

Cast-iron machine gun for shooting rolls of caps, double action, multi-shot, labeled in relief "ANTI-AIRCRAFT RAPID FIRE MACHINE GUN" and "RAPID FIRE MACHINE GUN," with olive-green stock and barrel and red handle, pivoting and semi-rotating on red stand with attenuated rear support and two front wheels; chamber of gun contains pin for cap roll and anvil and hammer turned by trigger-handle at side. Labeled in relief "GREY IRON CASTING CO. MT. JOY. PA.," etc.

44-6 Tank Cannon
Arcade Mfg. Co.
Freeport, IL, c. 1920
8" x 4¼" x 4¼"

Green cast-iron tank with orange and red decorations, open-work detail on bottom, cockpit with opening top and small hollow cannon; set on four wide-tread wheels; hole within cockpit for igniting firecracker. Labeled "AN ARCADE TOY MADE IN U.S.A." and impressed "ARCADE" and "U.S.A."

44-7 "Fire Cracker Cannon" Mortar
Kilgore Mfg. Co.
Westerville, OH, c. 1920
3¾" x 2½" x 3"

Cannon mortar with fat red iron barrel three-quarters-rotating on yellow iron stand; barrel hollow with hole in bottom for igniting firecracker. Labeled in relief with "K" in circle and "Kilgore."

45 | Optical Mechanical Toys

The toys in this category illustrate several themes which intrigued the Victorians: technological development, improvement of devices for educational purposes, and the possibilities of family entertainment in a domestic setting.

Most of the optical toys of the latter half of the nineteenth century began with two basic sources: the magic lantern or stereopticon, a rudimentary version of today's slide projector (see color illustration) and the phenomenon of "the persistence of vision," where a succession of images is presented at such a speed that the eye of the viewer cannot perceive the lapses between them, but rather "translates" them into one flowing and moving picture. The two sources were to be successfully combined in the cinematograph or motion picture machine at the end of the century.

The list of these devices is a long one, full of tongue-twisting "scientific" words: "thaumatrope," "phenakistoscope," "zoetrope," "periphanoscope," and so forth—each one claiming to be a great advance over all of its predecessors, and all quite remarkable to see in action.

French and German inventors are credited with the development of many of these toys, and indeed great numbers of the devices were imported from Europe. American manufacturers also capitalized on the optical toy craze, however, and models made in this country can also be found. Finally, the collector should know that many a "handy" father also took a crack at producing optical toys and that these also show up on the market, sometimes with manufactured parts from other toys. And, finally, yes, there are outright fakes abounding. If you would like to make some yourself, a delightful book, **Making Victorian Kinetic Toys** (see bibliography), is recommended; it also contains an excellent history of these toys with an explanation of exactly how many of them work—in much greater detail than is possible here.

The kaleidoscope (45-3) deserves a few words to itself. Compared to some of the other devices, it is a simple machine consisting of scraps of colored glass or other objects reflected into symmetrical visual arrangements through the use of two angled mirrors and viewed through a tube device against a light. But the simple beauty of the no-two-alike changing forms continues to fascinate even the most jaded television-watcher of today, and models are still being produced.

45-O Magic Lantern (Stereopticon) (color plate)
Maker undetermined
Possibly Germany, c. 1880-1910
8" x 4" x 12"

Detachable orange tin lantern with black and gilt striping and brass top and bottom; brass kerosene lamp, screwed to wooden stand; black tin brace, cylinder with glass back lens decorated in relief with satyr figure; detachable black tin slide holder; brass lens cylinder with glass front lens; black tin lantern chimney with brass rim. Pictures on slides are projected onto screen when lamp is lighted.

45-1 "Polyrama" Viewing Box
Maker undetermined
France, c. 1855
10" x 6¼" x 5"

Wooden box in shape of camera, with glass lens on paper accordion front moved back and forth by wooden handle. Printed and lithographed paper slides of various scenic views. Pictures on slides dissolve from daytime to nighttime when doors are opened and closed. Labeled "POLYRAMA."

45-2 "The Zoetrope"
Milton Bradley Co.
Springfield, MA, c. 1873
Toy: Diam. 2½", H. 2½";
     cylinder: Diam. 4¼", H. 3½"

Optical toy composed of circular wooden stand and wooden and steel pedestal for rotating cylinder; cylinder with wooden bottom labeled "THE ZOETROPE," with black cardboard sides with tin rims and vertically-cut narrow slots around perimeter. Slots create the impression of moving picture when serial strip is placed along inside edges of cylinder and cylinder is spun. Labeled "THE ZOETROPE" and "Milton Bradley Co., Springfield, Mass."

45-3 Kaleidoscope on Wooden
     Stand
Maker undetermined
U.S.A. or Germany, c. 1875
L. 10", H. 13½"

Leather-covered cylinder, containing lens, with glass-covered viewing hole at one end and brass rim at other end holding revolving translucent glass-covered cylinder containing multi-colored glass rods and water-filled glass tubes; container revolved by means of projecting brass spokes around circumference. Tumbling glass rods and tubes form ten-sided radially symmetrical designs viewed through lens within kaleidoscope cylinder.

45-4 Phenakistiscope
Maker undetermined
U.S.A. or Germany, c. 1880-1910
Handle: L. 8", W. 6½"; first disk:
   Diam. 8½"; second disk,
   Diam. 6½"

Optical toy consisting of wooden handle with brass pronged brace twisted around copper axle with circular cardboard disk rotating at each end; one disk with vertically-cut narrow slots around perimeter and second disk with series pictures of sailor tempting jumping dog with food. Dog appears to jump for food in sailor's hand when spinning picture disk is viewed through slots of spinning plain disk.

45-5 "Whirligig of Life"
McLoughlin Bros.
New York, NY, c. 1890
Periphanoscope: Diam. 5¾",
   H. 6¾"; tub: Diam . 8½", H. 4"

"Periphanoscope," with circular brown wooden stand and wooden and steel pedestal, labeled on bottom with printed paper directions entitled "WHIRLIGIG OF LIFE."; circular black tin tub with gilt trim, mirrored pillar at center, and hole in bottom to fit onto pedestal. Mirrors create the impression of moving pictures when serial strip is placed along inside edge of tub and tub is spun.

45-6 Reflector-Scope
Maker undetermined
Possibly Germany, c. 1900
H. 6¾"

Optical toy consisting of cardboard tube with lithograph of boy in sailor's clothes playing with toy ship and crew; three tin reflectors forming triangular cylinder inside, with glass and tin covers at each end, one with viewing hole.

45-7 "The New Mechanical Cinema"
Georg Levy
Nuremberg, Germany, c. 1920-30
W. 4½", H. 9½"

Optical toy composed of yellow tin hoop rotating vertically on steel rod set into steel clockwork; hoop contains tin slide holder also rotating on rod; hoop decorated with lithographed depiction of head of smiling boy; slides, consisting of four cardboard plates attached and folded at edges, individually printed on both sides with silhouettes of four pairs of consecutive scenes. Silhouetted figures appear to move when clockwork is wound to spin hoop. Labeled "GERMANY" and clockwork impressed "PW."

46 | Dioramas, Panoramas, and Toy Theaters

Another category of late-nineteenth-century visual toy is that containing the simpler and more static "picture shows," where no complicated machinery or optical tricks are employed—the toy theaters, dioramas, panoramas, and the like.

The basic concept is to reproduce a pictorial dramatic presentation in miniature, which is exactly what the miniature theater in the color illustration does: depth of field is gained by a simple layering of cut-out figures which are set up according to directions which come with the toy. The "Port de Mer" scene (46-2) is a slightly more complicated version, the same idea with more variation possible in movement and lighting.

Another version is the panorama (46-5), where a long paper strip with continuous or successive printed scenes is unrolled at one end and rerolled at another, passing by an opening for viewing.

Finally, there is the mechanical diorama, a scene with movable parts, often of cardboard, which are activated by the dropping of sand, by a clockwork device, or by manual shaking. (See illustrations 43-1, 43-3, 43-4, and 43-6). These toys may seem rather simple-minded to today's electronic game addict—but in their day, they apparently gave their viewers hours of amusement, for they were produced in great number.

These toys, when found, are likely to be in far less than mint condition since the cardboard and other light-weight materials from which they were made tend to deteriorate, but alterations, repairs, and "improvements" can usually be detected upon close examination. And the collector should not be too concerned if an acquisition is not in perfect working order, for the appeal of these toys lies in their depiction of Victorian values and humor more than in any mechanical qualities that they might exhibit.

46-0 "Theatre Royal" (color plate)
J.H. Singer and Mayer, Merkel & Ottmann
New York, NY, c. 1890
12" x 9¼" x 2" (folded)

Elaborate miniature theatrical setting with wooden stage, impressed "THEATRE ROYAL," and ornately lithographed paper-on-cardboard proscenium arch with linen curtain, surrounding Cinderella palace ball scene. Various characters are numbered, lettered and keyed into setting. Several layers of characters and props give illusion of depth and perspective. Impressed on stage "PAT FEB 88."

46-1 Black Man Dancing to Two Musicians
Maker undetermined
Possibly France, England, or Germany, c. 1850-75
9" x 2½" x 7"

Sand toy containing printed and hand-colored dining room scene with black violinist and banjo player and cut-out paper black dancer; musicians' playing arms and dancing figure connected by wire to sand mechanism behind scene. Dancer bounces up and down and musicians play instruments when box is turned twice to the left to activate sand mechanism. Paper label on back printed "MECHANICAL BOX WITH AUTOMATON" with complete directions for its use, and ending with "ROBERT LINK, Mechanician."

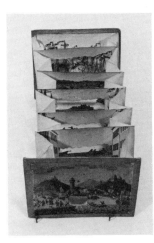

46-2 "Port De Mer"
Maker undetermined
Possibly France, Germany, or England, c. 1870
6" x 5" x 12" (when open)

Front cardboard plate labeled "PORT DE MER. Seehafen. SEAPORT." with paper picture of lighthouse and piers and with viewing hole with hinged door; back cardboard plate with paper picture of ships at port; plates connected by accordion-like white crepe sides with five paper prosceniums-and-wings with street and harbor scenes set at intervals between the sides. Series of prosceniums create depth of field when back plate is viewed through viewing hole.

46-3 Punch and Judy
Maker undetermined
Possibly England or Germany, c. 1870
7" x 8¼" x 2¾"

Lithographed scene of children and pipe player in audience, puppet theater, and figures of Punch and Judy swinging on nail axles inserted at stage floor. Punch and Judy bounce and concealed bells jingle when toy is rocked.

**46-4 Tailor Shop
A. Schoenhut Co.
Philadelphia, PA, c. 1875-95
18" x 5" x 13¾"**

Scene depicts tailor's shop with lithographed paper figures of seated boy, bearded tailor, boy ironing. Brass and steel clockwork connected by wires to figures. Figures sew and iron, tailor falls asleep, first boy lifts arm with needle to prick tailor awake, and tailor opens eyes and mouth in shock when clockwork is activated. Labeled "TRADE MARK" with insignia of Schoenhut Co.

**46-5 "Panorama of the Visit of Santa Claus to the Happy Children"
Milton Bradley & Co.
Springfield, MA, c. 1880
8¼" x 2" x 5¼"**

Cardboard box covered with black paper with display hole cut in front and bordered by pictures of Santa Claus, containing two wooden rollers turning paper scroll lithographed with pictures of children at play; lecture titled "Santa Claus' Panorama," with descriptions of each scene from Santa Claus's perspective and ads for other Milton Bradley toys on back. Labeled on box cover "PUBLISHED BY MILTON BRADLEY & CO. SPRINGFIELD. MASS."

46-6 Man with Umbrella Ringing Doorbell
Maker undetermined
U.S.A. or Germany, c. 1880-1900
9½" x 4¼" x 11½"

Diorama with lithographed scene of rain-soaked town street consisting of two layers with buildings and gaslight in back and door to building at front; two lithographed cut paper figures, one a sailor moving between building and street layers and one a gentleman with jointed arms and legs. Music box plays "Silent Night" when wound, and gentleman leans back and forth pulling doorbell and sailor ducks back and forth behind building when clockwork is activated.

47 | Historical Toys

Toys depicting military heroes and political figures and toys commemorating national events have been made throughout the nineteenth and twentieth centuries, and collecting such toys can be challenging and educational.

These "historical" toys are of types which have been discussed in earlier categories—automatons, cap guns and exploders, lithographed wooden toys, bell toys, cannons and airplanes—but they have been singled out here for special attention since their chief interest is the event or personality portrayed—and the attitude of the toymaker toward that event or personality—which is most important.

In some cases, famous people seem to have been used as the models for toys simply to add to their salability with no particular attitude taken toward the celebrity. This is the case with the General Grant figure illustrated in color; any automaton which actually smoked a cigar would be appealing, but this one all the more so since the prototype figure is someone famous. To be contrasted with this is the "Woman's Rights Advocate" automaton (47-5), where the main point is not the action (which is really not very complex or interesting) but in the social commentary which the toymaker was setting forth here about the women's rights movement and blacks rather than about a specific personality. The toy strikes one today as almost vicious, but it sold very well in the white-male dominated 1890s. Both toys, by the way, were manufactured by Ives.

The Centennial of 1876 and the Columbian Exposition of 1893, perhaps the two greatest national celebrations ever, provided toy manufacturers with further subject matter on which to capitalize. Washington-worship reappeared in many forms and toys commemorating the Revolution were made in great quantity (47-2, 47-3). The Columbus toys of the 1890s were more elaborate and fanciful (47-6), and Spanish-American War toys generally followed their pattern (47-7).

The twentieth century had its heroes and events to commemorate, too—for example, the Teddy Roosevelt and Panama Canal toys, which appeared in several forms (47-8, 36-2). And then there was Lindbergh and the "Spirit of St. Louis" (47-9).

Another kind of "historical" toy, those made with the idea of inculcating "American" values through the teaching of American history —for instance those made by the Milton Bradley Company of Springfield, Massachusetts: "Bradley's Historiscope" and "Panorama of American History"—were also popular at home as well as in the classroom.

47-0 General Grant Smoking Cigar (color plate)
Ives, Blakeslee & Co.
Bridgeport, CT, c. 1875-85
9" x 5¼" x 13¾"

Elaborate automaton character figure representing General Ulysses S. Grant, with detailed cast-iron head and hands, stuffed torso in pewter-buttoned blue uniform; figure sits cross-legged on cast-iron chair, holding brass funnel-cigar. Clockwork mechanism in base (which also contains a coin-slot and bank receptacle) moves head of figure and hand with cigar; when mechanism is wound and smoke device activated, smoke is blown from mouth of figure when cigar removed.

47-1 General Butler
Ives, Blakeslee and Co.
Bridgeport, CT, c. 1875
H. 9½"

Animated doll-type figure of Civil War General Benjamin Butler, with cast-iron head, hands, and shoes and cloth uniform with brass buttons; clockwork inside body. Doll strides forward on rollers when clockwork is wound. Impressed "PATD. SEPT. 21. 75."

47-2 George Washington Cap Bomb (left)
Maker undetermined
U.S.A., c. 1876
H. 1½"

Nickel-plated cast-iron cap bomb, single shot, in shape of Washington's head, made up of upper and lower halves held together by spring along vertical groove from neck to temples and head; hook at top of head. Washington was the most popular historical figure to appear on American toys, and there was a great revival in "historical" toys, such as this one, at the time of the Centennial of the American Revolution.

"1776" Revolver (right)
J. and E. Stevens Co.
Cromwell, CT, c. 1876
H. 5¼"

Bronze cap revolver, labeled in relief "1776" and "1876," single action, single shot, with stationary cylinder, decorated in relief with concentric circles and vine on stock and stars and frill border on handle. This gun was made in great quantity at the time of the Centennial.

47-3 "Ye Hero of '76"
Charles M. Crandall
Montrose, PA, c. 1876
H. 8"

Flat lithographed wood representation of Revolutionary War soldier with jointed limbs, which is set into grooves in wooden stand in various positions. From an advertisement: "Shows how the enemy skedaddled," "imitates a Broadway Swell," etc. Centennial toy.

47-4 Gladstone and Palmerston Wrestling
Maker undetermined
Germany or England, c. 1880
Figures: 7" x 2¼" x 8¾"

Detailed painted wooden and papier-mâché figures of English political rivals William Gladstone and Viscount Palmerston, dressed in
period cloth costumes; flat-cut wooden arms and legs joined in realistic wrestling pose; mounted on stand of wood with steel rods from
which figures are suspended. "Jumping-jack" figures bounce and
"wrestle" when stand is shaken.

47-5 "Woman's Rights" Clock-work Figure
Ives, Blakeslee & Co.
Bridgeport, CT, c. 1890-93
5" x 4" x 10½"

Caricature figure set on wooden
base containing clockwork
mechanism; doll representing
black woman as an advocate for
women's rights, depicted with
glazed eyes, wide-open mouth,
and exaggerated tongue and
teeth standing with tin folder before wooden lectern with leather-
bound wooden book; papier-
mâché head, wooden torso, flat-
cut tin arms and hands jointed at
shoulders, cotton and silk cloth-
ing. Doll leans forward over lectern and bangs right hand on top.
[Today one might differ with the
1893 Ives catalog which pro-
claimed that "These toys when
wound produce a great deal of
amusement; their movements are
very comical." Toys which showed
derisive attitudes toward women
and blacks were common; this
one does both.]

47-6 "Landing of Columbus" Bell Toy
J. and E. Stevens Co.
Cromwell, CT, c. 1890-1910
6¾" x 3½" x 5½"

Gilded cast-iron boat, labeled in relief "Landing of Columbus," decorated with floral designs, lion figure-head, and crucifix banner; figures of four sailors and standing figure of Columbus with standard; set on two back wheels and one front balancing wheel. When toy is pulled, clapper on back axle rings bell at stern of boat.

47-7 "Dewey" Cannon
Kenton Hardware Mfg. Co.
Kenton, OH, c. 1899
11½" x 5¼" x 6"

Varnished cast-iron firecracker cannon partially rotating on frame decorated with bas-relief bust of Spanish-American War Admiral George Dewey; stars-and-stripes motif and simulated hobnails. Labeled "DEWEY" and "KENTON BRAND."

47-8 Teddy Roosevelt Figure
A. Schoenhut Co.
Philadelphia, PA, c. 1908
H. 8½"

Caricature figure depicting President Theodore Roosevelt in safari outfit (including wooden helmet and leather belt and pouch) and pince-nez glasses. Materials used include wood, papier-mâché, cotton, leather, and rubber. This was the first spring-jointed character figure made by Schoenhut and was part of an elaborate 53-piece set called "Teddy's Adventures in Africa."

**47-9 "Spirit of St. Louis" Yellow
    Airplane
J. Chein & Co.
New York, NY, c. 1926
8" x 7" x 2¾"**

Yellow lithographed tin and steel
airplane, with red markings labeled "Spirit of St. Louis" on nose
and "N-X-211" on tail, with rotating blade at front; set on two blue
wheels. Steel barrel-and-spring
mechanism inside. Airplane rolls
forward when mechanism is
wound.

48 | Comic Strip Toys

Comic strip toys have enjoyed a collecting boom over the past
several years and entire books have been devoted to them. As one
might expect, they are among the most colorful, action-packed,
and humorous of toys.

Comic strips appeared at the very end of the 1890s and comic
strip toys were not far behind. The Yellow Kid, said to be the first comic strip, appeared in 1896 and we soon find him in the form of a cap
bomb and riding in a cast-iron goat cart; the Katzenjammer Kids appeared the next year and shortly thereafter appeared in bell toys,
horse-drawn carts, and banks. And so it went with succeeding comic strips right up to the present. The comic strips represented in the illustrations and other entries are familiar to most readers. **Comic Strip
Toys** by Kenny Harman (see bibliography) is an invaluable aid to collectors interested in these toys. The Disney toys are perhaps the most
numerous; Mickey Mouse, especially, appears in hundreds of
models.

The extent to which German manufacturers capitalized on the
comic strip craze is quite remarkable, though less so after one
realizes that German toys, the cheaper ones particularly, practically flooded the American market in the twenty years or so preceding
World War I and to a lesser extent in the period between the two
World Wars. German toys of this caliber were also designed for other
non-German markets, changing their personalities from country to
country.

The Toonerville Trolley, from the Fontaine Fox comic strip of that
name, is one of the most often encountered comic strip toys. It came
in numerous variations, some of which are illustrated here (48-2); in
fact, these trolley varieties are sufficiently numerous that the collector would do well to check carefully before buying—there are fakes
among them. "The Powerful Katrinka" comes from the same comic

strip in the model shown here (48-3) and in a model with Jimmy in a wheelbarrow.

Comic strip toys illustrate better than any other type of toy the marked impact of newspapers and other media on the tastes and ways of thinking of Americans in the early twentieth century. They are philosophically a far cry from the nineteenth-century matter-of-fact work-ethic toy.

48-O "Mickey Mouse" Hand Organ (color plate)
Probably Johann Distler
Nuremberg, Germany, c. 1930
6" x 2¾" x 8"

Polychrome-lithographed tin hand organ, labeled "MICKEY MOUSE" on front and with various comic scenes of Mickey on back and sides, and set on two red wheels with steel axle; Mickey, set in harness comprised of several molded and flat-cut pieces attached to steel and lead crank at side of organ. Minnie Mouse, made of two molded halves clasped together set on vertical steel rod inserted into top of organ. Steel clockwork inside organ. Mickey cranks handle while rocking back and forth, Minnie bounces up and down, and music box plays plink-plonk sounds when clockwork is wound.

**48-1 Max and Moritz on
    Reversible Flat Spiraled Pole
Maker undetermined
Germany, c. 1905
5" x 2" x 8¼"**

Two flat-cut painted and lithographed figures of Max and Moritz, one with black hair and one with blonde hair, dressed in schoolboys' clothes, each rotating on either end of double strip sliding up and down on flat-cut spiraled strip set between two blue platform disks. Max and Moritz rotate upright and rock back and forth down spiral strip, either face to face or back to back, each time toy is tipped.

48-2 "Toonerville Trolley" with Skipper (left)
Maker undetermined
Possibly Nifty
Germany, c. 1922
5" x 2½" x 7½"

Lithographed tin red and yellow trolley with black trim, smokestack at top, three arch-cut windows on each side; set on four gray wheels, one back wheel off-center; flat-cut Skipper at front control-rod; clockwork beneath body. Trolley rolls forward, then shakes, and Skipper shakes control rod when clockwork is wound. Labeled "TOONERVILLE TROLLEY."

Orange "Toonerville" Trolley with Smoke (center)
Maker undetermined
Germany, c. 1923
3" x 1¼" x 3½"

Painted pot metal orange trolley, with silver trim, silver Skipper at front and silver passenger at back, trolley set on four chartreuse wheels; simulated smoke at top made of wire and cotton. Labeled "TOONERVILLE."

Green "Toonerville" Trolley and Skipper (right)
Dent Hardware Co.
Fullerton, PA, c. 1920
4" x 2" x 6¼"

Nickel-plated and cast-iron trolley, painted bright green with orange trim, three arch-cut windows on each side, smokestack and trolley wire at top, platform at front and back, flat-relief Skipper at control rod; set on four nickel-plated wheels, one back wheel off-center. Trolley rolls forward, up and down, when top is pulled. Labeled in gilt relief "TOONERVILLE."

48-3 "The Powerful Katrinka"
Nifty
Germany, c. 1923
H. 5¼"

Humorous stocky Katrinka character, stamped "THE POWERFUL KATRINKA," made of two molded lithographed tin halves clasped together, dressed in blue checked blouse and white apron, with movable arms, and set on three wheels, right arm connected to small boy, Jimmy, made of two molded halves clasped together. Katrinka rolls forward, singlehandedly lifting Jimmy, when interior clockwork is wound. Labeled "MADE IN GERMANY. G.M. 34282" and "COPYRIGHT 1923 BY FONTAINE FOX PAT. APPLIED FOR No. 297049."

48-4 Maggie and Jiggs on Cart
Nifty
Germany, c. 1924
7" x 2½" x 5½"

Lithographed tin Jiggs, labeled "JIGGS", dressed in striped pants, tails and top hat, with movable arms, one holding cane; and Maggie, with cat, dressed in long spotted skirt and red blouse, with movable arms, one holding rolling pin; both figures made of two molded halves clasped together and attached to either end of cart resting on four wheels and joined in the middle by flexible band of tin. Cart rolls, and Maggie and Jiggs bounce and battle when clockwork is wound. Labeled "MADE IN GERMANY" and "COPYRIGHT 1924 BY INTERNAT'L FEATURE SYNDICATE. GEO McMANUS."

48-5 Andy Gump "348" Roadster
Arcade Mfg. Co.
Freeport, IL, c. 1924-28
7" x 3½" x 6"

Painted cast-iron red roadster with rotating crank, gas cap, set on four green simulated tires; Andy Gump, in high collar, gloves and green hat sits at red steering wheel. Labeled in relief "348."

48-6 Felix The Cat
Maker undetermined
Possibly U.S.A., c. 1925
H. 4"

Felix, black wood, stamped "FELIX" across chest, with rubber cord jointed limbs, spiral-jointed tail, black leather ears, and white face.

48-7 Felix The Cat on Scooter
Nifty
Germany, c. 1930
7¼" x 3" x 6"

Lithographed and painted tin Felix, made of two molded halves clasped together, labeled on tail "FELIX," black, with white face and movable arms; attached to orange scooter. Felix pumps handle and scooter moves forward when clockwork is wound.

48-8 Mickey Mouse with Drum
Probably Nifty
Germany, c. 1930
H. 6½"

Mickey Mouse, flat-cut tin with movable arms, attached to drum on front labeled "Mickey Mouse" and to spring-and-gear mechanism on back. Fan with weights inside drum revolves hitting top of drum, and Mickey's arms reverberate off drum when geared handle on mechanism is pressed down on spring to turn gears.

48-9 Moon Mullins and Kayo
**   Handcar**
Louis Marx and Co.
New York, NY, c. 1932
6" x 2½" x 6½"

Gray lithographed tin and steel handcar with black brace at center supporting partially rotating black axle with steel handlebars and attached by vertical strip to rod on gear inside car; car supporting flat tin jointed figures of Moon Mullins and Kayo on either end of car attached at hands to handlebars, Kayo on top of simulated wooden box labeled "XXX DYNAMITE DANGER" and "48 STICKS DO NOT JAR," car set on four flanged wheels, one pair adjustable for circling barrel-spring and gears inside car. Mullins and Kayo pump handle when car is run crackling along track or floor when mechanism is wound.

48-10 "Donald Duck Handcar"
Lionel Corp.
New York, NY, c. 1935
10½" x 3½" x 6¼"

Sheet metal handcar and green and white metal doghouse set on red metal platform on four flanged wheels; doghouse contains composition Pluto with bouncing head and black paper ears; composition Donald Duck standing behind house with movable arms attached to handle which Donald "pumps" when clockwork toy is wound.

48-11 Popeye on "Patrol" Motor-cycle
Hubley Mfg. Co.
Lancaster, PA, c. 1938
8" x 2¼" x 4"

Painted cast-iron red motorcycle, with molded headlight, back light, and joints; fenders and spokes set over two rubber tires with tin spokes, tab of tin attached to front fender striking spokes of front wheel, balanced on two small white rubber wheels; cast-iron Popeye sits on top. Labeled in relief "PATROL."

49 | More Simple Toys

Throughout the period under discussion, there were always cheaper, simpler toys on the market than many of those discussed in the preceding sections, and many of these appear on the toy market today but are difficult to identify and classify and hard to value. Four categories of this type of toy have been chosen here for illustrative purposes—and each is a collectible category in its own right.

"Penny toys" are just that: toys which originally cost one cent. Today some of them bring several hundred dollars. In general, they are rough miniature copies of the larger, more expensive toys, often made of tin. In other words, they are cousins twice removed from the "real thing:" a regular toy steam engine copies a real steam engine; a penny toy steam engine copies the toy steam engine, and so forth. It was the closest that many children came to the more elaborate toys.

Roly-polies are rather crudely made and finished "Humpty Dumpty" type toys which have heavy rounded bottoms, as the name suggests. They are made of papier-mâché or plaster of Paris and often are three-dimensional caricatures of assorted types. They rock back and forth, refusing to turn over, when moved. The Schoenhut models are especially collectible.

Nodders are another type of balancing toy, typically composed of a base with a wooden stick protruding upward on which a separate hollowed-out papier-mâché head rests and rocks back and forth. These too are usually caricature toys, are also rather crudely fashioned, and originally sold very cheaply.

Finally, there are Tootsie toys—which might be called the royalty of simple toys. There are entire collections devoted to them, and there is no doubting their appeal to many collectors. These are die-cast or slush-cast (as distinguished from sand-cast) toys, usually vehicles, which began to be made in about 1910. The most collectible of them are the earlier die-cast models (the slush-cast ones are rough and are easy to fake), the specialty models (such as the 1932 "funnies" series), and the custom livery models bearing names of various stores which ordered them for advertising purposes.

49-O Mustachioed Clown (Roly Poly) (color plate, right)
A. Schoenhut Co.
Philadelphia, PA, c. 1908
H. 4½"

Painted papier-mâché clown, with black hair and mustache, dressed in gray peaked hat and red ruff and shirt; rocking on black base. Linen label on bottom printed "SCHOENHUT 'ROLLY DOLLY' PATENTED DEC. [13?]. 1908. Other Patents Pending."

"Police Patrol" Wagon (Tootsie Toy) (color plate, lower right)
Dowst Mfg. Co.
Chicago, IL, c. 1932
L. 2½"

Blue die-cast metal police patrol wagon from "Moon Mullins" comic strip, with solid movable wheels and steel axles and colorful printed figures of Moon Mullins and policeman.

Humpty Dumpty (Nodder) (color plate, left)
Maker undetermined
Germany, c. 1890-1910
H. 4½"

Papier-mâché Humpty Dumpty, with blue eyes on head bouncing on wire spring on wooden post set into pair of blue and yellow boots on maroon wooden disk. Stamped on bottom "D.R.G.M. 363. . . ."

Monkey Riding Dog on Cradle (Penny Toy) (color plate, center)
Maker undetermined
Germany, c. 1910
3" x 1" x 3½"

Lithographed tin uniformed monkey riding white dog on rocker cradle set on band of green tin connected to bend in axle of back wheels of green platform; monkey and dog rock when toy is pulled. Impressed "GES. GESCH."

49-1 Penny Toys

Gilt Dog Pulling Blue Wagon (upper left)
Maker undetermined
Possibly Germany, c. 1910
6" x 1½" x 2"

Gilt tin dog with slash-cut eyes attached by blue shafts to luminous blue and red wagon embossed with decorative detail.

Fire Engine (lower left)
Maker undetermined
Germany, France, or England, c. 1910

Gilded and lithographed tin fire engine with cylinder, red and white carriage, and driver in blue uniform and gilded helmet.

Steam Engine (center)
Maker undetermined
Germany, France, or England, c. 1910
H. 4", D. 2¼"

Gilded and black and orange painted tin steam engine on dome base containing two pulley wheels on parallel axles. Lead wheel revolves and rod moves in and out of cylinder when pulley handle is turned.

Taxi (upper right)
Maker undetermined
Germany, France, or England, c. 1910
4½" x 2" x 2½"

Blue and yellow lithographed tin taxi, with articulated driver and flat-cut passengers; clockwork mechanism beneath body.

Chemical Truck (lower right)
Maker undetermined
Germany, France, or England, c. 1910
3¾" x 1" x 2"

Blue lithographed tin truck with red engine and semi-cylindrical back; ladders in relief, seated driver.

49-2 Roly Polies (from left to right)

Clown in Lavender Suit
Maker undetermined
Germany, c. 1930
H. 3¾"

Painted papier-mâché clown with white face decorated in blue, and dressed in green peaked hat and lavender collar and suit, rocking on lavender base.

Baby with White Cap and Blue Bow Tie
A. Schoenhut Co.
Philadelphia, PA, c. 1904
H. 4¼"

Painted papier-mâché baby dressed in white cap with blue bow tie at chin, and in white shirt, rocking on yellow base.

Clown with Crocheted Ruff
Maker undetermined
Germany, c. 1930
H. 3½"

Papier-mâché clown dressed in cream-colored shirt with three large gilt buttons, blue, gilt and red vest, black top hat, and cotton crocheted ruff, rocking on green base. Inscribed "32/47 15L."

Sea Captain
Maker undetermined
Germany, c. 1910-30
H. 5"

Painted papier-mâché sea captain with chin-beard and shoulder-length wig, dressed in black three-corner hat, blue-green coat and yellow waistcoat with shirt frill, rocking on orange base.

Bird in Black Top Hat and Red Jacket
Maker undetermined
Germany, c. 1910-30
H. 4"

Painted celluloid yellow bird, holding black cane, dressed in black top hat, red jacket, black tie and white waistcoat and pants, rocking on white and simulated green grass base.

49-3 Nodders (from left to right)

Clown in Black Skull Cap
Maker undetermined
Germany, c. 1890-1910
H. 7"

Wire and painted cardboard clown figure in blue suit, white and red polka-dotted tie, and black skull cap. Body has dowel on top on which head balances.

Brown-Haired Schoolboy in Cap
Maker undetermined
Germany, c. 1890-1910
H. 5"

Papier-mâché schoolboy dressed in blue patched pants, pullover and cap, with brown hair, one glass eyeball and one winking eye, and white face on head bouncing on wire spring at wooden neck.

Pumpkin-Head in Green Cap
Maker undetermined
Germany, c. 1890-1910
H. 5½"

Papier-mâché pumpkin-head dressed in red suit, with orange face, green peaked cap and blue feathered mustache on head bouncing on wire spring at wooden neck. Stamped on bottom "MADE IN GERMANY."

Sailor Boy
Maker undetermined
Germany, c. 1890-1910
H. 4¾"

Papier-mâché sailor boy, dressed in blue sailor's suit and hat, with blue pop-eyed pink face on head swinging on wire at wooden neck.

Policeman
Maker undetermined
Germany, c. 1890-1910
H. 6¼"

Papier-mâché policeman dressed in blue uniform with conical helmet, pink face with blue eyes and brown mustache on head swinging on wire at pink wooden neck; set on brown wooden disk.

49-4 Tootsie Toys "Funnies" Series
Dowst Mfg. Co.
Chicago, IL, c. 1932
L. each approximately 2½"

Die-cast metal pull-toy vehicles, including "KO Ice" truck and Mamie boat, each with solid movable wheels and steel axles with colorfully painted comic figures, also of die-cast metal. From the 1932 catalog: "Nationally famous newspaper comic characters are now reproduced as Toostie toys. . . .Imagine Moon Mullins or Smitty in action!"

50 | Extravaganzas

And now the toys for the child (or toy collector) who has everything—and who can afford more! These are the cream of the toy manufacturers' production: extravagant, carefully designed and finished, and rare.

These toys have other qualities in common—a shared interest in animation and in the personality of the figures. They each have a story to tell in addition to the actions which they perform.

Without further ado, here they are. They speak for themselves.

50-O House on Fire with Firemen and Women (color plate)
Francis W. Carpenter
Port Chester, NY, c. 1892
12¼" x 9" x 20¾"

Representation of house on fire, on wooden stand, with brown wooden walls and painted cast-iron brick façade, gilt molding and painted flames, fireman figure in relief at window. Elaborate pulley mechanism with gilt tin elevator traveling in shaft inside house. Woman on wheels "escapes" down shaft, thereby lifting cast-iron fireman who "rescues" second woman by hooked arms off balcony to roof. Labeled in relief "PATENTED JAN 19 1892."

50-1 Doll on Bicycle Track
Althof Bergmann and Co.
New York, NY, c. 1870
Diam. 19½", H. 10"

Doll with parian-ware head and flat tin jointed limbs, dressed in blue wool coat and white bloomers, on bicycle with grooved wheels; connected by bent rod to clockwork inside red tin case on finished wooden base at center of circular open-work blue tin track. Doll rides bicycle around track when clockwork is wound.

50-2 Five Bisque Clowns Playing Instruments on Box
Maker undetermined
Possibly France, c. 1900
8" x 24½" x 13¾"

Doll figures of clown musicians, each with bisque head with blue glass eyes, white hair wig, open mouth with teeth and wooden hands. Musicians play various instruments (trumpets, mandolin, violin and guitar) and music box plays melody when clockwork inside base is wound.

50-3 Acrobat-and-Globe Tower
Fernand Martin
Paris, France, c. 1903
Diam. 4", H. 16"

Tin tower, set on open-work pedestal with pink and white slide spir-aling around central pole, with circus flag at top; tin acrobat jointed at waist attached to inside of each half of opening hollow globe; globe connected by rod to string and rotating spring inside pole; string wrapped around wooden handle. Globe is pulled down to bottom of slide by string, then rolls back up slide top-like with rotating spring, and opens to reveal acrobat. Labeled "F.M. PARIS JOUET BTE. S.G.D.G. FRANCE ET ETRANGER DRGM 269-877."

50-4 "Ajax" Tumbler
Ernst Lehmann
Brandenburg, Germany, c. 1908
H. 9¼"

Robot-like figure labeled "AJAX," dressed in white and gilt tights, blue slippers and red and gilt helmet labeled with Lehmann insignia and with "MARKE" and "DRGM," holding two brown clubs and standing on two simulated wooden skis; steel barrel spring in-

side torso. Tumbler does backward somersaults, using clubs
and skis as stands, when mechanism is wound. Labeled "MARKE
LEHMANN," etc., with patent
dates.

**50-5 Swan and Zeppelin with
    Palace Straddling Tub
Maker undetermined
Possibly Germany, c. 1910
Diam. 12", H. 13"**

Gray and red painted tin palace,
with central cylinder and arches
on either side, soldered to opposite edges of perimeter of green
tub; gray zeppelin, projecting on
rod from flagstaff with circus flag,
and white swan, projecting on rod
from beneath cylinder; clockwork
inside cylinder. When clockwork is
activated, swan swims in water in
tub and zeppelin circles above.

**50-6 Clown Drawing at Easel
Maker undetermined
Germany, c. 1910
5½" x 5" x 5¼"**

Brown steel platform supporting
lithographed tin clown with pencil
seated on box in front of easel with
arms and neck connected to
mechanism inside platform; steel
handle at side. Clown nods and
draws picture of self with pencil on
paper placed on easel when handle is cranked.

50-7 "Hi-Way Henry"
Maker undetermined
Germany, c. 1927
10" x 4" x 8¾"

Lithographed and painted tin jalopy, labeled "HI-WAY HENRY," with yellow body, canopy-like orange roof set on four red posts, lithographed banners on each side listing tourist sites, and dog-house in engine labeled "HENRY IV"; many other comic elements; wind-up mechanism within car. Car rolls forward, shakes and rattles and rises at rear off ground when mechanism is activated. Labeled "COPYRIGHT BY OSCAR HITT" and "MADE IN GERMANY." Hi-Way Henry was a well-known comic-strip character.

50-8 "Marx Merrymakers" Mice
Band
Louis Marx and Co.
New York, NY, c. 1932
9" x 5½" x 9"

Lithographed tin piano, labeled "MARX MERRYMAKERS," red, white and black, decorated with music and pictures of mice behind bars; connected by rods to four tin mice, with movable wire arms and legs, in black, white, and red dinner jackets, one conducting, one playing drums with cat's face, one at piano, and one standing as if singing. Barrel and spring mechanism inside piano. Labeled "MARX TOYS TRADE MARK LOUIS MARX & CO. . . . ."

Acknowledgments

First and foremost, I wish to thank the staff of the Perelman Antique Toy Museum, particularly Leon J. Perelman, for resources and help. I owe a special debt to Dee Andrews, former Curator, who compiled much of the basic information as to identification and attribution of makers, dates of manufacture, and so forth. Appreciation is also due John Fell and Cindy Haveson of the Museum for their aid.

Thanks also go to collectors Dennis Milstein and John Willard who gave me the benefit of their knowledge and judgment in special areas. Janis Watson and Patricia Harris typed the manuscript, and decoded my handwriting, with expertise and an undue degree of good-naturedness. Finally, I wish to thank my daughter and son, Ellen Ayres and James Ayres, for their enthusiasm, encouragement, and unremunerated assistance.

All of the toys in this book were photographed at the Perelman Antique Toy Museum, Philadelphia, Pennsylvania, by J. Michael Kanouff.

About the Perelman Antique Toy Museum

Located in the center of Philadelphia's fashionable Society Hill section, and within a few blocks of Independence Hall, is the historic Abercrombie House (270 South 2nd Street), built in 1758 by Capt. James Abercrombie, Sr., a noted seaman. Handsomely restored, the building now houses one of the most complete and unusual collections of toys in America—the Perelman Antique Toy Museum.

On three floors, visitors can see massed displays of American toys, representing two centuries of "history in miniature." Although every type of toy is on display, the museum is particularly noted for its collection of mechanical and still banks, the largest in the world; a wide assortment of automatons, each of which features one or more mechanical actions; a rare collection of animated cap pistols; and a particularly varied (and very large) collection of toy vehicles—from fire engines and stagecoaches to hansom cabs and gigs—that, taken together, tells the entire history of American transportation in toys.

Although the Perelman Museum is only one of Philadelphia's many historical and cultural treasures, it is the one museum that cannot be missed by anyone seriously interested in toys or in the history of American childhood.

Selected Bibliography

Bailey, Carolyn Sherwin. *Tops and Whistles.* New York: Viking Press, 1937.

Barenholtz, Bernard, and Inez McClintock. *American Antique Toys, 1830-1900.* New York: Harry Abrams, Inc., 1980.

Barenholtz, Edith, ed. *The George Brown Toy Sketchbook.* Princeton, NJ: The Pyne Press, 1971.

Bartholomew, Charles. *Mechanical Toys.* Secaucus, NJ: Chartwell Books, 1979.

Bauman, Paul. *Collecting Antique Marbles.* Leon, IA: Prairie Winds Press, 1970.

Best, Charles, N. *Cast Iron Toy Pistols, 1870-1940.* Englewood, CO: Rocky Mountain Arms and Antiques, 1973.

Buser, M. Elaine and Dan Buser, Schoenhut's Dolls, Toys and Circus. Paducah, KY: Collector Books, 1976.

Cadbury, Betty. *Playthings Past.* New York: Praeger Publishers, 1976.

Chapuis, Droz. *Automata.* New York: Central Book Co., 1958.

Culff, Robert .*The World of Toys.* New York: Hamlyn, 1969.

Daiken, Leslie. *Children's Toys Throughout the Ages.* London: Spring Books, 1963.

Fraser, Antonia. *A History of Toys.* London: Delacorte Press, 1966.

Foley, Dan. *Toys Through the Ages.* Philadelphia: Chilton Publishers, 1962.

Freeman, Ruth, and Larry Freeman. *Cavalcade of Toys.* New York: Century House, 1942.

Gordon, Leslie, *Peepshow into Paradise.* New York: John DeGraff, Inc., 1953.

Grober, Karl. *Children's Toys of Bygone Days.* New York: Frederick Stokes Co., 1928,

Harman, Kenny. *Comic Strip Toys.* Des Moines, IA: Wallace-Homestead Book Co., 1975.

Hertz, Louis H. *Collecting Model Trains.* Wethersfield, CT: Mark Haber & Co., 1956.

_____. *The Handbook of Old American Toys.* Wethersfield, CT: Mark Haber & Co., 1947.

_____. *Messrs. Ives of Bridgeport.* Wethersfield, CT: Mark Haber & Co., 1950.

_____. *Riding the Tinplate Rails.* Wethersfield, CT: Mark Haber & Co., 1944.

_____. *The Toy Collector.* New York: Funk & Wagnalls, 1969.

Hillier, Mary. *Pageant of Toys.* New York: Taplinger Publishing Co., 1966.

Holme, C. Geoffrey, *Children's Toys of Yesterday.* New York: Studio Publications, 1932.

King, Constance Eileen. *The Encyclopedia of Toys.* New York: Crown Publishers, 1978.

Long, Earnest A., and Ida Long. *Dictionary of Toys Sold in Amrica.* [U.S.A.]: 1971 (Vol. I), 1978 (Vol. II).

McClintock, Inez, and Marshall McClintock. *Toys in America.* Washington, DC: Public Affairs Press, 1961.

McClinton, Katharine Morrison. *Antiques of American Childhood.* New York: Bramhall House, 1970.

Milet, Jacques, and Robert Forbes. *Toy Boats (1870-1955).* New York: Charles Scribner's Sons, 1979.

Miller, Robert. *Price Guide to Toys.* Des Moines, IA: Wallace-Homestead Book Co., 1975.

Murray, Patrick. *Toys.* London: Studio Vista, Ltd., 1968.

O'Brien, Richard. *Collecting Toys.* Florence, AL: Books Americana, Inc., 1979.

Pearsall, Ronald. *Collecting Mechanical Antiques.* New York: Arco Publishing Co., 1973.

Pressland, David. *The Art of the Tin Toy.* New York: Crown Publishers, 1976.

Sayer, Philip, and Caroline Sayer. *Making Victorian Kinetic Toys.* New York: Taplinger Publishing Co., 1977.

Schorr, Martyn L. *The Guide to Mechanical Toy Collecting.* Haworth, NJ: Performance Media, 1979.

Schroeder, James, J., Jr., ed. *Toys, Games and Dolls.* Chicago: Follett Publishing Co., 1971.

Spong, Neldred, and Raymond Spong. *Flywheel Powered Toys.* [U.S.A.]: Antique Toy Collectors of America, 1979.

White, Gwen. *Antique Toys and Their Background.* New York: Arco Publishing Co., 1971.

_____. *Toys and Dolls, Marks and Labels.* Newton, MA: Charles T. Branford Co., 1975.

Whitton, Blair. *Bliss Toys and Doll Houses.* New York: Dover Publications, 1979.

Index